THE WORLD AROUND

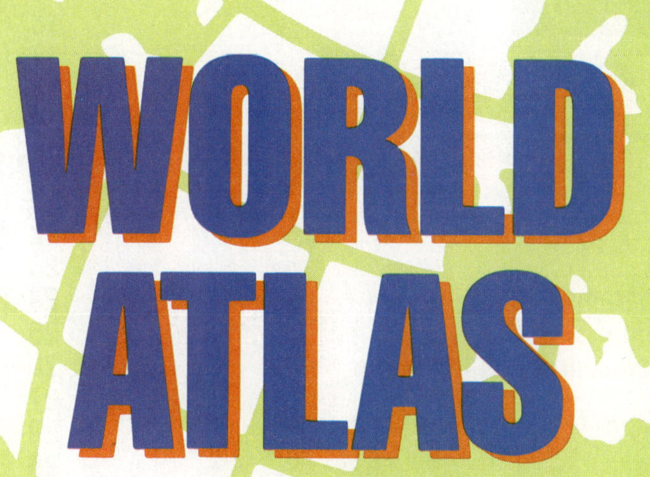

WORLD ATLAS

for intermediate students

MACMILLAN/McGRAW-HILL SCHOOL PUBLISHING COMPANY
NEW YORK CHICAGO COLUMBUS

CONTENTS

PAGE iv — THE WORLD

PAGE 12 — THE UNITED STATES AND CANADA

PAGE 32 — LATIN AMERICA

PAGE 40 — EUROPE AND NORTHERN ASIA

PAGE 48 — THE MIDDLE EAST AND NORTH AFRICA

CHARTS AND GRAPHS

The World

The earth is home to many different groups of people. People live in many different ways throughout the world, but we all share the same planet.

Imagine that you are an astronaut peering down at Planet Earth from your spaceship. What does the world look like from so high in the sky? One astronaut, Neil Armstrong, has said that from space the earth looks like a "tiny pea, pretty and blue."

From space the world's mountains, deserts, and other landforms look small and almost trivial. On the earth, however, they do much to shape the way we live. People all over the world use the land to meet their basic needs and wants. Because the

The earth moves around the sun at a speed of 67,000 miles (106,200 km) per hour.

AROUND THE WORLD IN ...

The earth is 24,000 miles (38,400 km) long at its center. A car can travel this distance in 18 days. According to the drawing, how long does it take a space shuttle to travel the same distance?

earth's landforms differ from place to place, people all over the world must work in different ways to meet their needs and wants.

As you look through this Atlas, or book of maps, keep in mind that no two places in the world are exactly alike. Think about what makes places throughout the world similar and different—things such as climate, landforms, and natural resources. Then think about how such things affect people and the way they live.

Oceans, mountains, deserts, and rain forests shape the way people live throughout the world.

Planet Earth looks like this from space.

THE EARTH

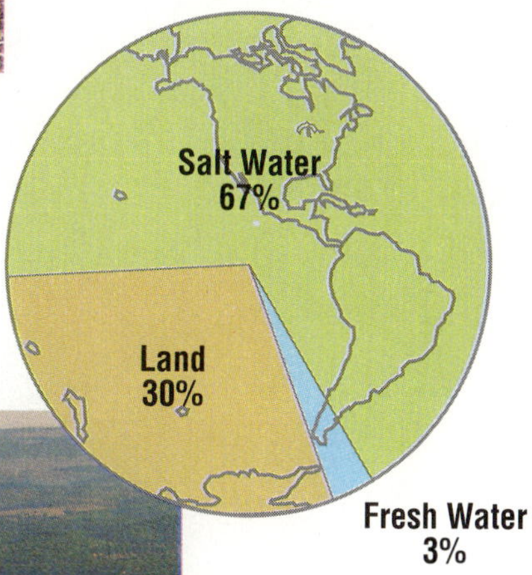

According to the circle graph, how much of the earth is covered by water? Some of this water is contained in pretty lakes such as the one below.

THE WORLD
Physical

ARCTIC OCEAN
Arctic Circle
EUROPE
ALPS
Mont Blanc
15,771 ft. (4,807 m)
Volga R.
URAL MTS.
Ob River
Mt. Elbrus
18,510 ft.
(5,642 m)
ASIA
GOBI
HINDU KUSH
HIMALAYAS
Indus R.
Ganges R.
Chang R.
Mt. Everest
29,028 ft
(8,848 m)
SYRIAN DESERT
SAHARA
Nile R.
AFRICA
DECCAN PLATEAU
Tropic of Cancer
PACIFIC OCEAN
Equator
Mt. Kilimanjaro
19,340 ft. (5,895 m)
INDIAN OCEAN
NAMIB DESERT
KALAHARI DESERT
SOUTH ATLANTIC OCEAN
Cape of Good Hope
GREAT SANDY DESERT
AUSTRALIA
Tropic of Capricorn
Mt. Kosciusko
7,310 ft. (2,228 m)
0 1,000 2,000 Miles
0 1,000 2,000 3,000 Kilometers
Scale accurate at Equator
N
Antarctic Circle
ANTARCTICA

THE WORLD
Political

ABBREVIATION KEY

Abbreviation:	Country:
(FR.)	FRANCE
(GR.)	GREECE
(IT.)	ITALY
(NETH.)	NETHERLANDS
(NOR.)	NORWAY
(PORT.)	PORTUGAL
(S.A.)	SOUTH AFRICA
(SP.)	SPAIN
(U.K.)	UNITED KINGDOM
(U.S.)	UNITED STATES

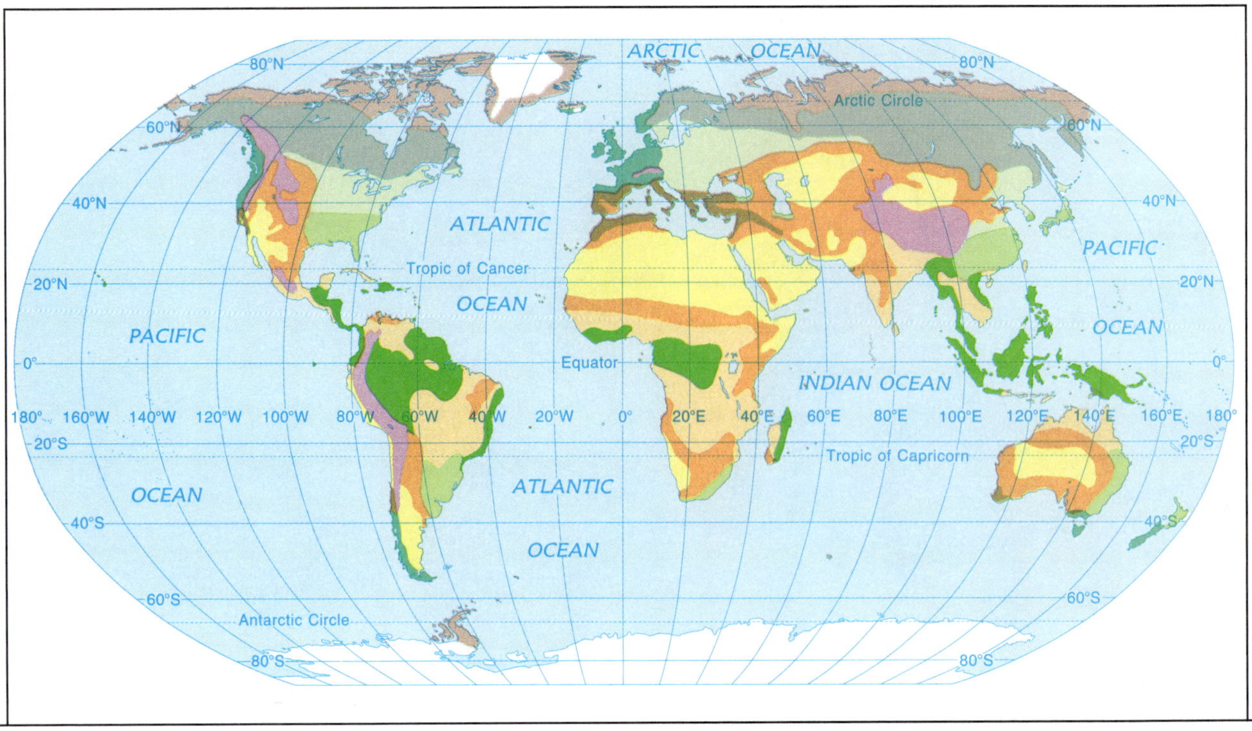

THE WORLD: Climate

- Ice cap
- Very cold winter, cold summer, dry
- Very cold winter, cool summer, wet
- Highlands, temperature and precipitation vary with elevation
- Semi-dry, temperature varies with latitude
- Cold winter, hot or warm summer, wet
- Mild winter, cool summer, wet
- Mild or warm winter, hot summer, wet
- Mild, wet winter; hot, dry summer
- Dry, temperature varies with latitude
- Warm all year, wet with one dry season
- Warm and wet all year

THE WORLD: Time Zones

Non-standard time

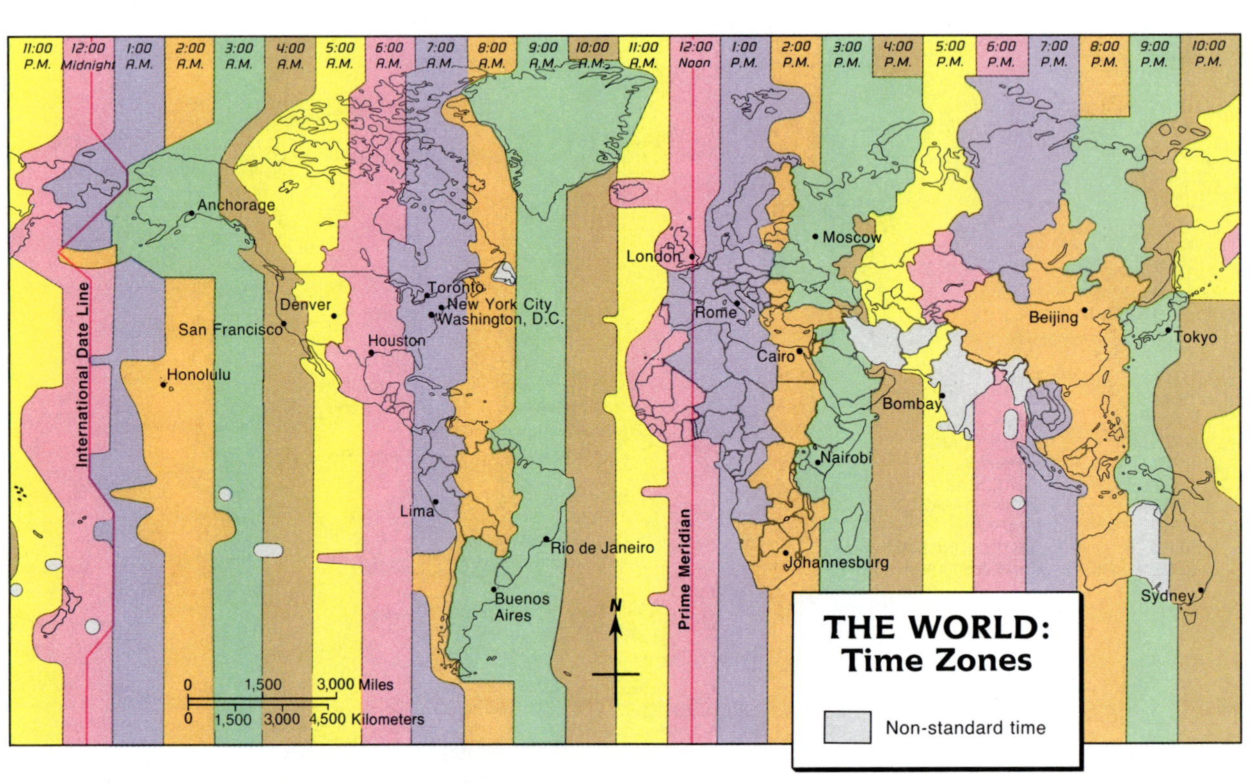

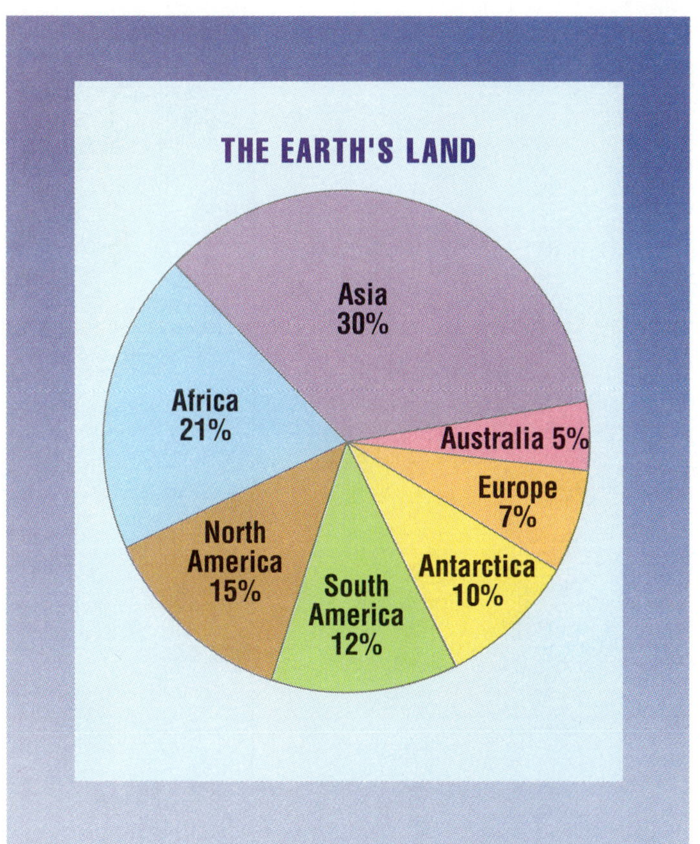
THE EARTH'S LAND
Asia 30%
Africa 21%
Australia 5%
Europe 7%
North America 15%
South America 12%
Antarctica 10%

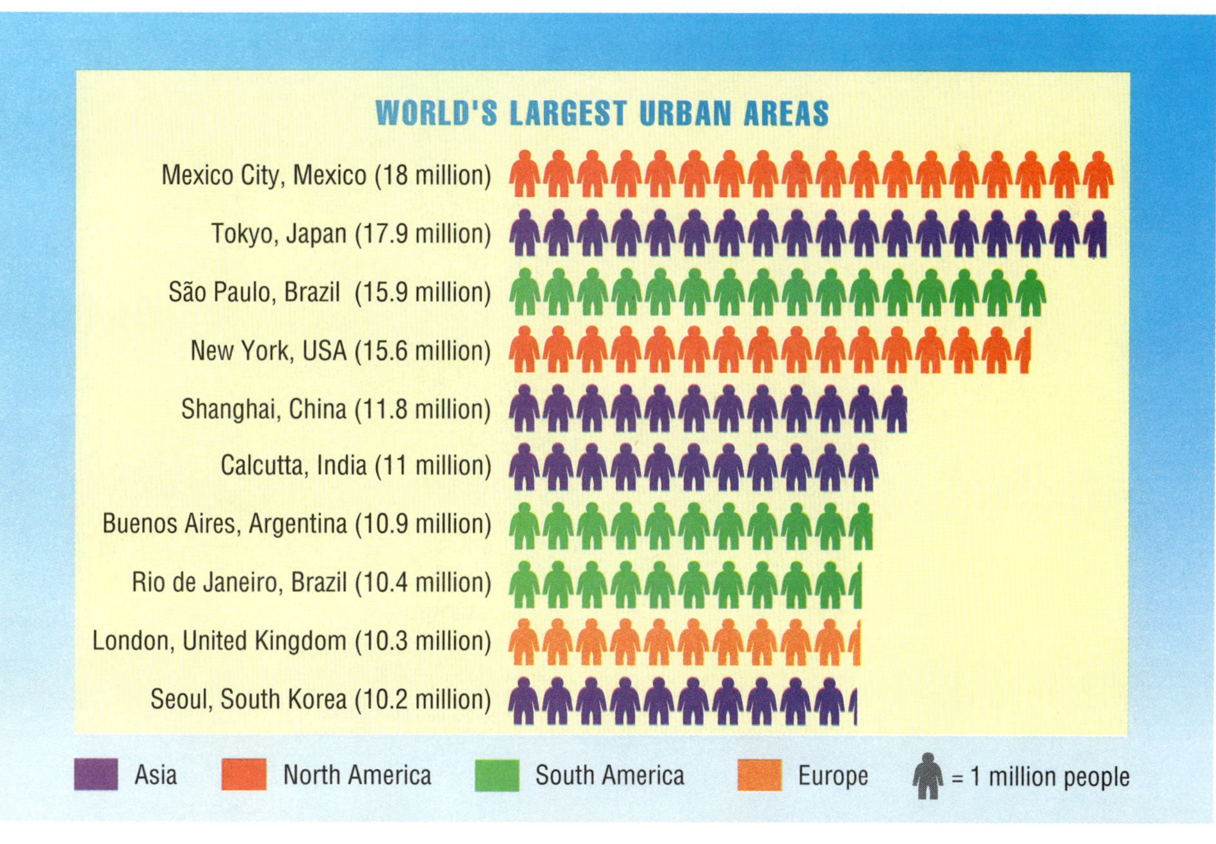
WORLD'S LARGEST URBAN AREAS
Mexico City, Mexico (18 million)
Tokyo, Japan (17.9 million)
São Paulo, Brazil (15.9 million)
New York, USA (15.6 million)
Shanghai, China (11.8 million)
Calcutta, India (11 million)
Buenos Aires, Argentina (10.9 million)
Rio de Janeiro, Brazil (10.4 million)
London, United Kingdom (10.3 million)
Seoul, South Korea (10.2 million)
Asia
North America
South America
Europe
= 1 million people

WORLD CARTOGRAM: Population

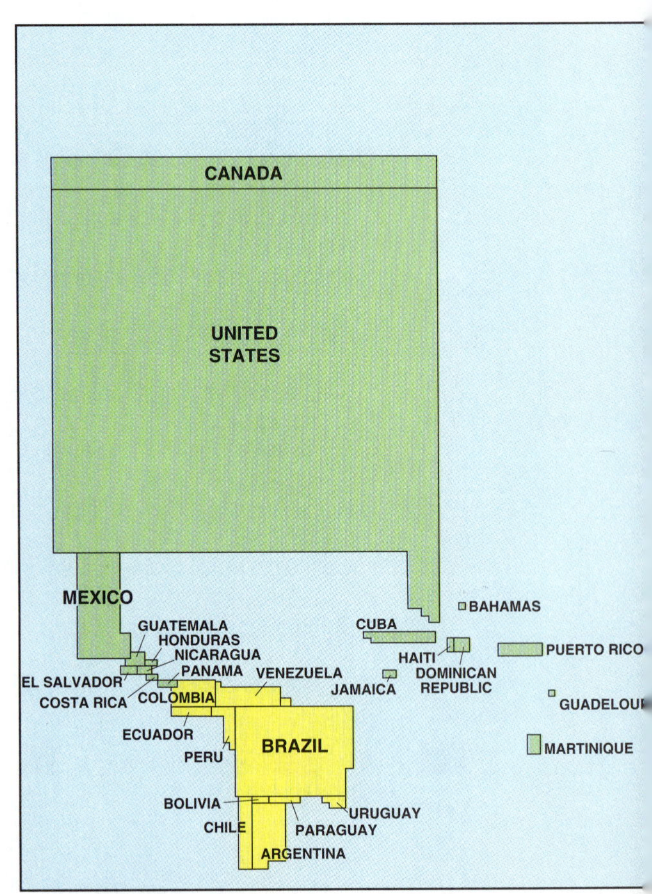

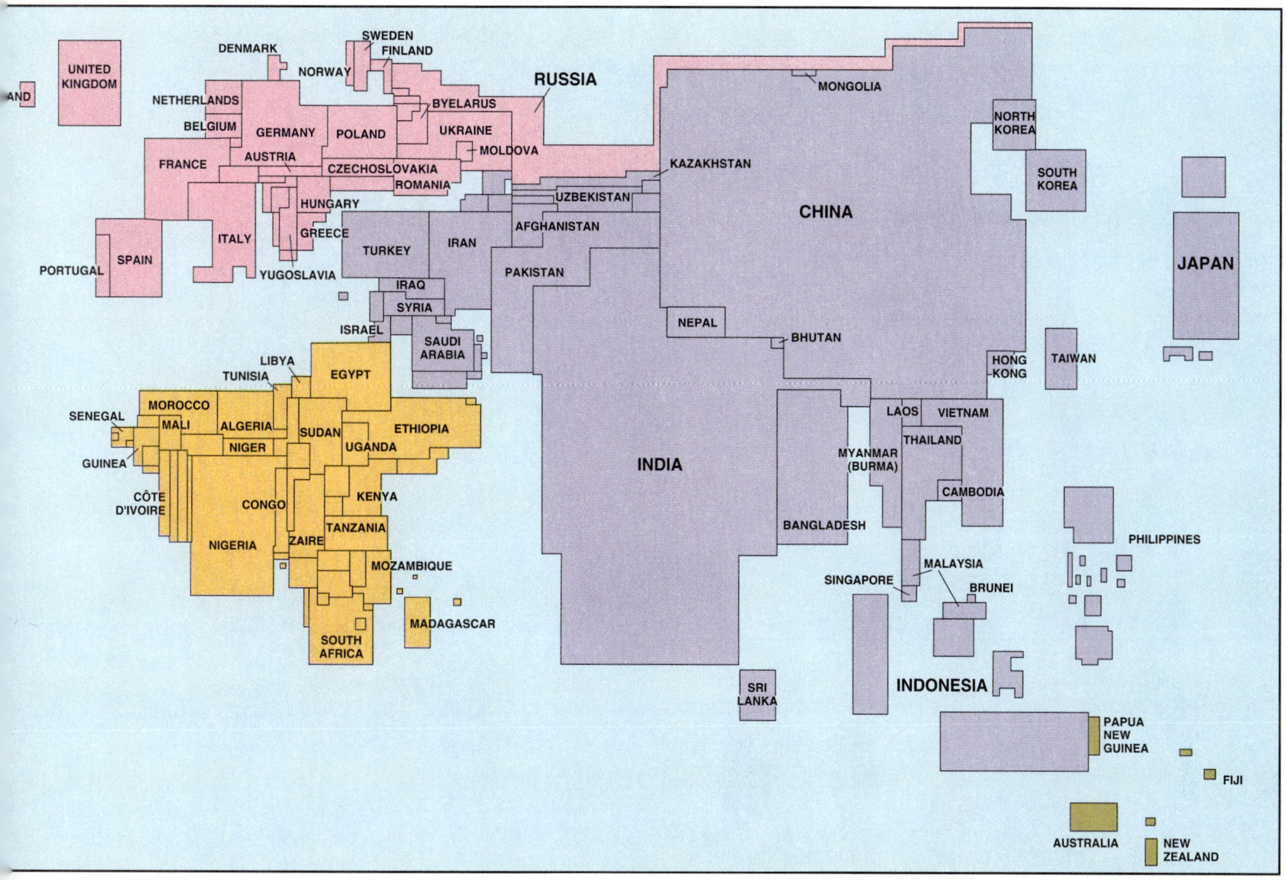

WORLD CARTOGRAM: Gross National Product

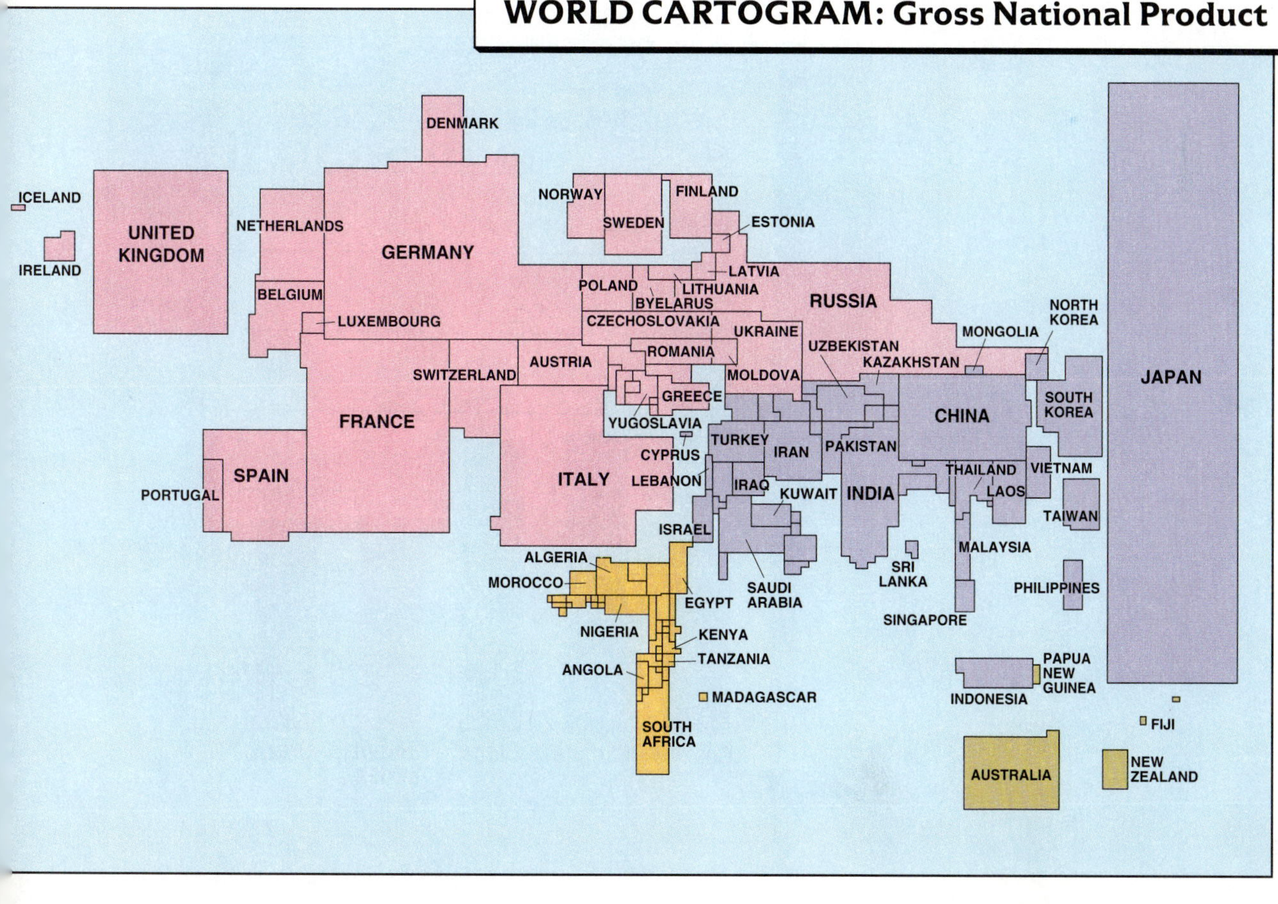

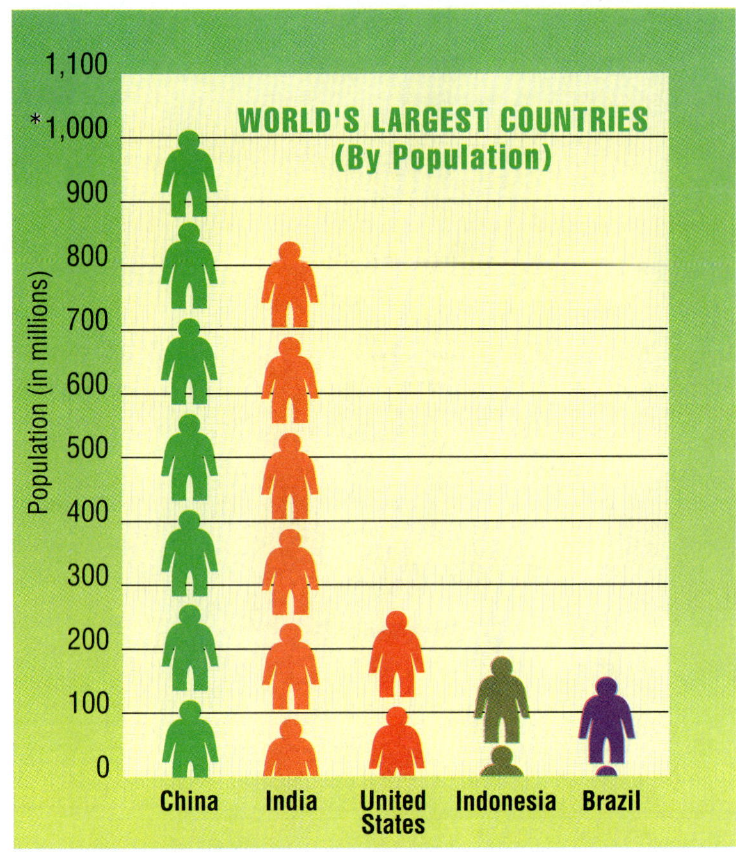

* 1,000 million = 1 billion

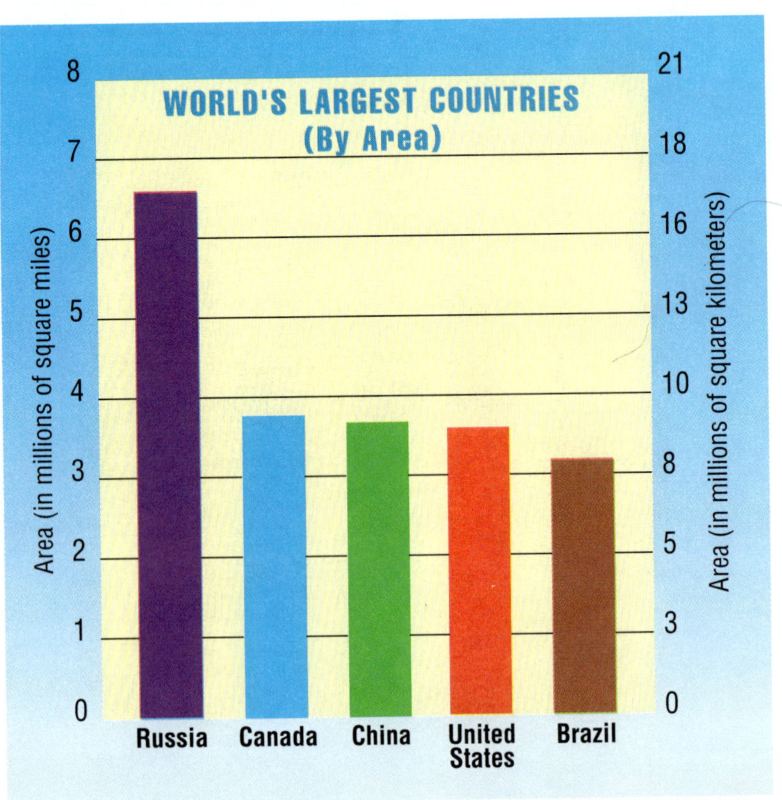

LONGEST RIVERS OF THE WORLD

River	Country	Length in miles (kilometers)
Nile	Egypt	4,100 miles (6,560 km)
Amazon	Brazil	4,000 miles (6,400 km)
Chang Jiang (Yangtze)	China	3,964 miles (6,342 km)
Mississippi-Missouri	United States	3,710 miles (5,936 km)
Ob	Russia	3,362 miles (5,379 km)
Huang (Yellow)	China	2,903 miles (4,644 km)
Congo	Zaire	2,900 miles (4,640 km)
Amur	Russia	2,744 miles (4,390 km)
Lena	Russia	2,734 miles (4,374 km)
Mackenzie	Canada	2,635 miles (4,216 km)
Mekong	China	2,600 miles (4,160 km)
Yenisey	Russia	2,543 miles (4,068 km)

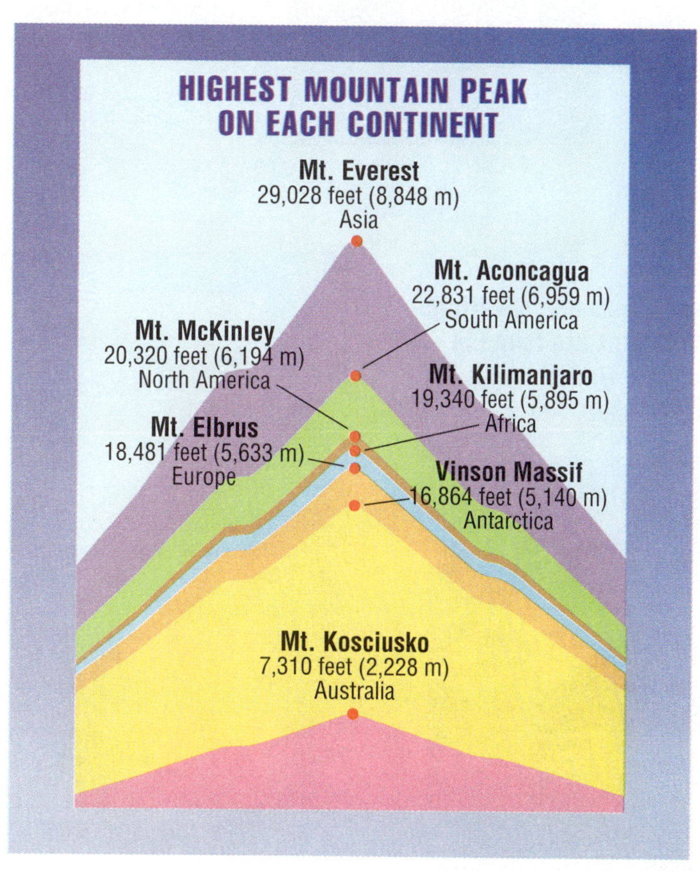

UNITED STATES AND CANADA

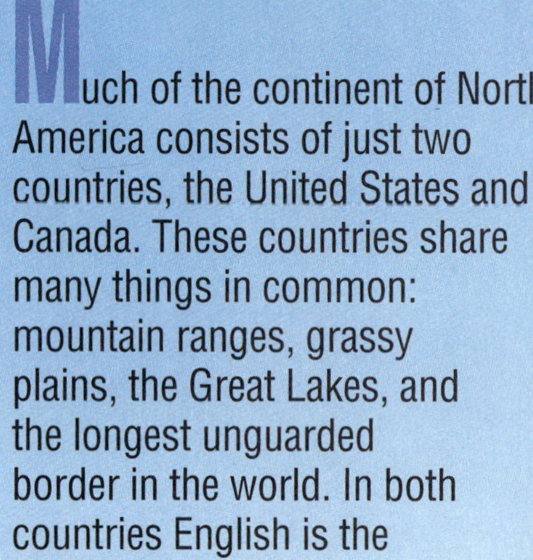

Much of the continent of North America consists of just two countries, the United States and Canada. These countries share many things in common: mountain ranges, grassy plains, the Great Lakes, and the longest unguarded border in the world. In both countries English is the principal language.

There are also many differences between the United States and Canada. The United States has almost ten times as many people as Canada,

People of many different backgrounds live in the countries of the United States and Canada.

Vast plains and towering mountains are found in both the United States and Canada.

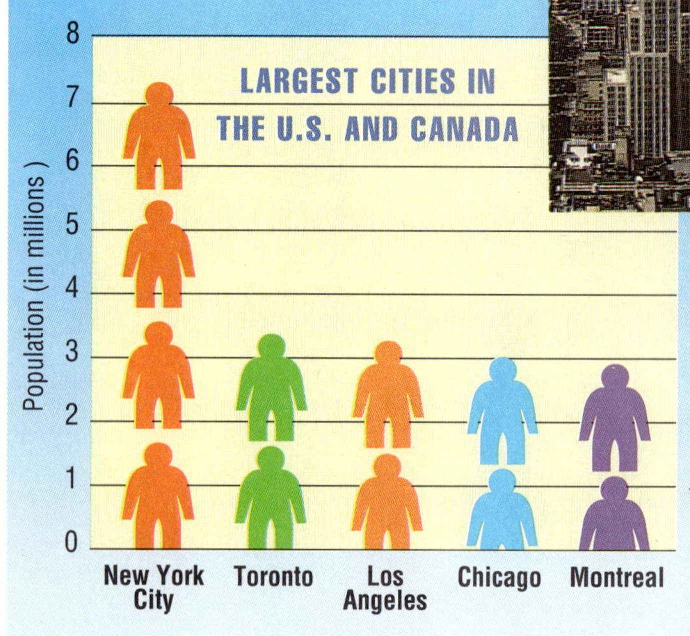

although Canada is a larger country. French is spoken in some areas of Canada. Forests cover much of Canada, whereas most forests in the United States have been cleared to make way for towns and cities. Canada's most important exports are forest products. In contrast, the most important exports of the United States are machinery and transportation equipment.

Take a close look at the maps of this region. Find as many differences as you can between the landforms that make up Canada and the United States. Then find as many similarities as you can between the two countries. Identify some of the common features of this region.

New York City (*left*) is the largest city in this region. According to the graph, what is the population of Toronto (*below*)?

The Great Lakes form the world's largest group of freshwater lakes.

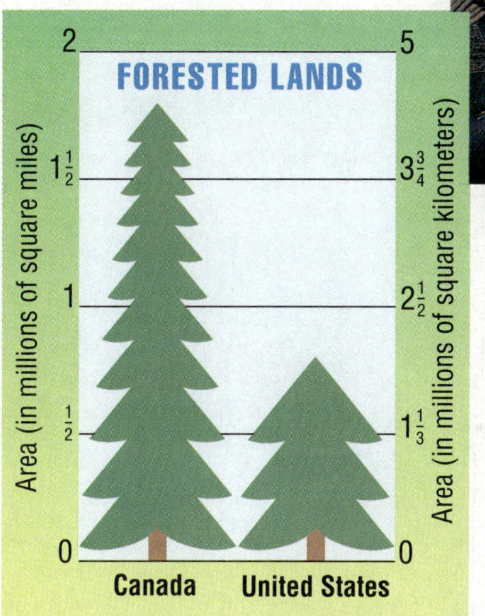

Forest products are Canada's most important export. According to the graph, which country contains more forested lands?

Both Canada and the United States have thousands of miles of beautiful coastland.

UNITED STATES AND CANADA
Physical
0 500 1,000 Miles
0 500 1,000 1,500 Kilometers
RUSSIA
ARCTIC OCEAN
Greenland
Queen Elizabeth Islands
Baffin Bay
Davis Strait
Arctic Circle
Baffin Island
Banks Island
Victoria Island
Beaufort Sea
Point Barrow
Bering Strait
Bering Sea
BROOKS RANGE
Yukon River
Mt. McKinley 20,320 ft. (6,194 m)
ALASKA RANGE
Alaska Peninsula
Gulf of Alaska
Great Bear Lake
Mackenzie River
Great Slave Lake
Lake Athabasca
Hudson Bay
Labrador Sea
Labrador
SHIELD
CANADIAN
Lake Winnipeg
Saskatchewan River
ROCKY MOUNTAINS
COAST MOUNTAINS
Fraser River
Vancouver Island
PACIFIC OCEAN
N
NORTH AMERICA
Gulf of St. Lawrence
St. Lawrence River
Nova Scotia
Lake Superior
Missouri River
GREAT PLAINS
INTERIOR PLAINS
L. Michigan
Lake Huron
Lake Ontario
Lake Erie
APPALACHIAN MOUNTAINS
Cape Cod
Long Island
CASCADE RANGE
Columbia R.
Snake River
Cape Mendocino
COAST RANGES
SIERRA NEVADA
GREAT BASIN
Great Salt Lake
Colorado River
Platte River
R.
Ohio River
Arkansas River
Mississippi
Red River
COASTAL PLAINS
ATLANTIC OCEAN
Rio Grande
Florida Peninsula
Gulf of Mexico
MEXICO
CUBA
Caribbean Sea
Tropic of Cancer
Hawaiian Islands
80°N
60°N
40°N
20°N
160°E
180°
160°W
140°W
120°W
100°W
80°W
60°W
40°W
20°W

UNITED STATES AND CANADA
Political
National capital
Provincial or state capital
Other city
0 500 1,000 Miles
0 500 1,000 1,500 Kilometers
RUSSIA
ARCTIC OCEAN
GREENLAND (DENMARK)
Ellesmere Island
Queen Elizabeth Islands
Banks Island
Victoria Island
Baffin Island
Beaufort Sea
Bering Sea
Davis Strait
Arctic Circle
ALASKA (U.S.)
Yukon River
YUKON TERRITORY
Whitehorse
Juneau
NORTHWEST TERRITORIES
Yellowknife
Great Bear Lake
Great Slave Lake
Mackenzie River
Hudson Bay
BRITISH COLUMBIA
Fraser River
Vancouver Island
Vancouver
Victoria
ALBERTA
Edmonton
Calgary
CANADA
SASKATCHEWAN
Saskatchewan River
Lake Athabasca
Regina
MANITOBA
Lake Winnipeg
Winnipeg
ONTARIO
Sudbury
Toronto
Kingston
Ottawa
Hull
Montreal
Quebec
QUEBEC
St. Lawrence River
NEWFOUNDLAND
St. John's
PRINCE EDWARD ISLAND
Charlottetown
NEW BRUNSWICK
Fredericton
NOVA SCOTIA
Halifax
PACIFIC OCEAN
N
WASHINGTON
Olympia
OREGON
Salem
Columbia R.
IDAHO
Boise
Snake River
MONTANA
Helena
WYOMING
Cheyenne
NEVADA
Carson City
CALIFORNIA
Sacramento
San Francisco
Los Angeles
UTAH
Salt Lake City
COLORADO
Denver
ARIZONA
Phoenix
Colorado River
NEW MEXICO
Santa Fe
NORTH DAKOTA
Bismarck
SOUTH DAKOTA
Pierre
Missouri R.
NEBRASKA
Lincoln
KANSAS
Topeka
Arkansas River
OKLAHOMA
Oklahoma City
Red River
TEXAS
Austin
Dallas
Houston
Rio Grande
UNITED STATES
MINNESOTA
St. Paul
Lake Superior
WISCONSIN
Madison
L. Michigan
IOWA
Des Moines
MO
Jefferson City
AR
Little Rock
LA
Baton Rouge
New Orleans
Mississippi
IL
Chicago
Springfield
IN
Indianapolis
MI
Lansing
Lake Huron
Lake Erie
Lake Ontario
OHIO
Columbus
KENTUCKY
Frankfort
TENNESSEE
Nashville
MS
Jackson
AL
Montgomery
GEORGIA
Atlanta
FLORIDA
Tallahassee
SOUTH CAROLINA
Columbia
NORTH CAROLINA
Raleigh
VIRGINIA
Richmond
WV
Charleston
Washington, D.C.
MD
Annapolis
DE
Dover
PA
Harrisburg
Philadelphia
NJ
Trenton
NY
Albany
New York City
CT
Hartford
RI
Providence
MA
Boston
VT
Montpelier
NH
Concord
MAINE
Augusta
ATLANTIC OCEAN
Gulf of Mexico
MEXICO
CUBA
Caribbean Sea
PUERTO RICO (U.S.)
Tropic of Cancer
Honolulu
HAWAII (U.S.)
80°N
60°N
40°N
20°N
160°E
180°
160°W
140°W
120°W
100°W
80°W
60°W
40°W
20°W

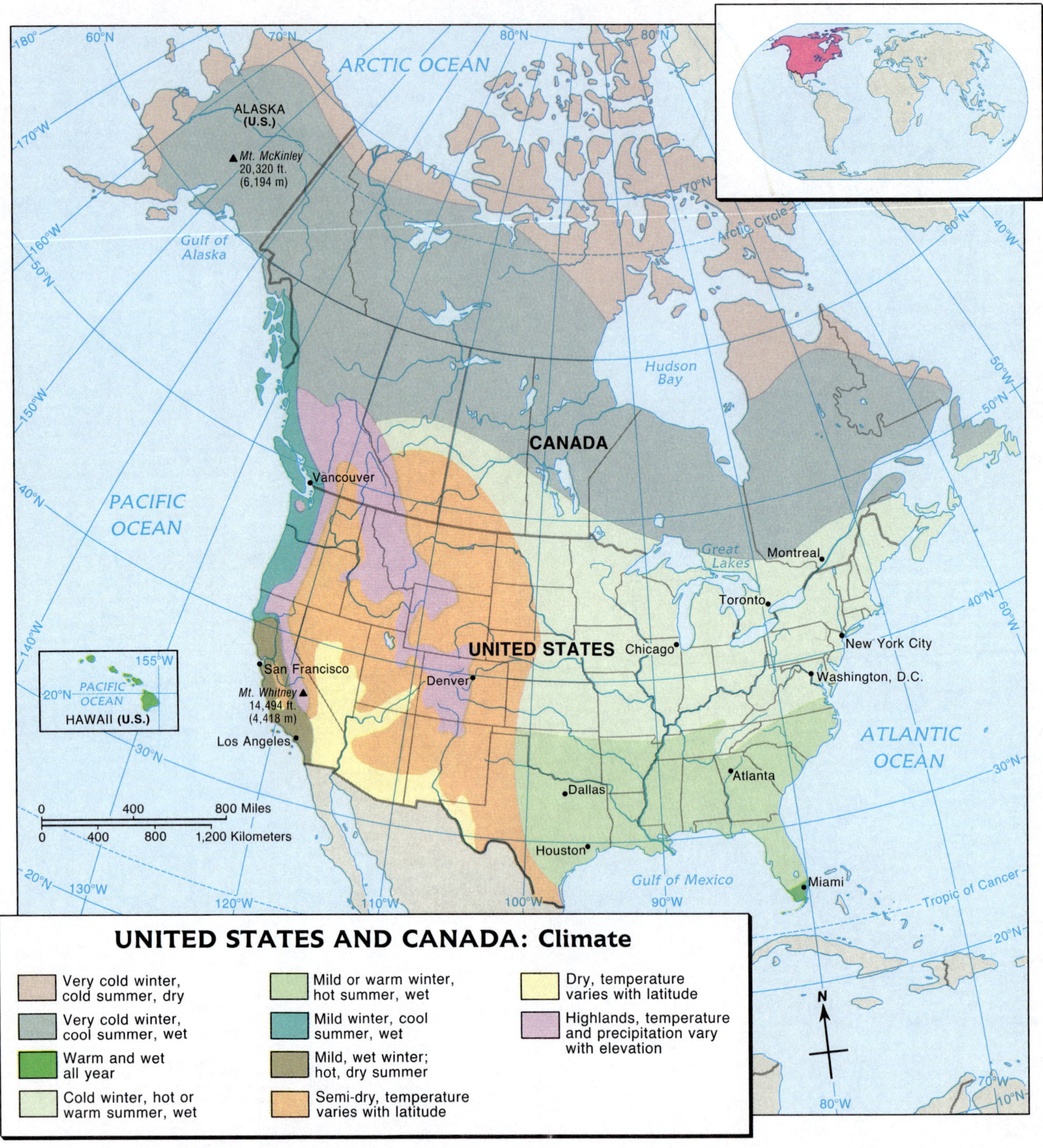

ARCTIC OCEAN
ALASKA (U.S.)
Mt. McKinley 20,320 ft. (6,194 m)
Gulf of Alaska
Hudson Bay
CANADA
PACIFIC OCEAN
Vancouver
Great Lakes
Montreal
Toronto
New York City
Chicago
UNITED STATES
Washington, D.C.
San Francisco
Denver
Mt. Whitney 14,494 ft. (4,418 m)
Los Angeles
PACIFIC OCEAN
HAWAII (U.S.)
ATLANTIC OCEAN
Atlanta
Dallas
Houston
Gulf of Mexico
Miami
Arctic Circle
Tropic of Cancer
0 400 800 Miles
0 400 800 1,200 Kilometers
N
UNITED STATES AND CANADA: Climate
Very cold winter, cold summer, dry
Very cold winter, cool summer, wet
Warm and wet all year
Cold winter, hot or warm summer, wet
Mild or warm winter, hot summer, wet
Mild winter, cool summer, wet
Mild, wet winter; hot, dry summer
Semi-dry, temperature varies with latitude
Dry, temperature varies with latitude
Highlands, temperature and precipitation vary with elevation

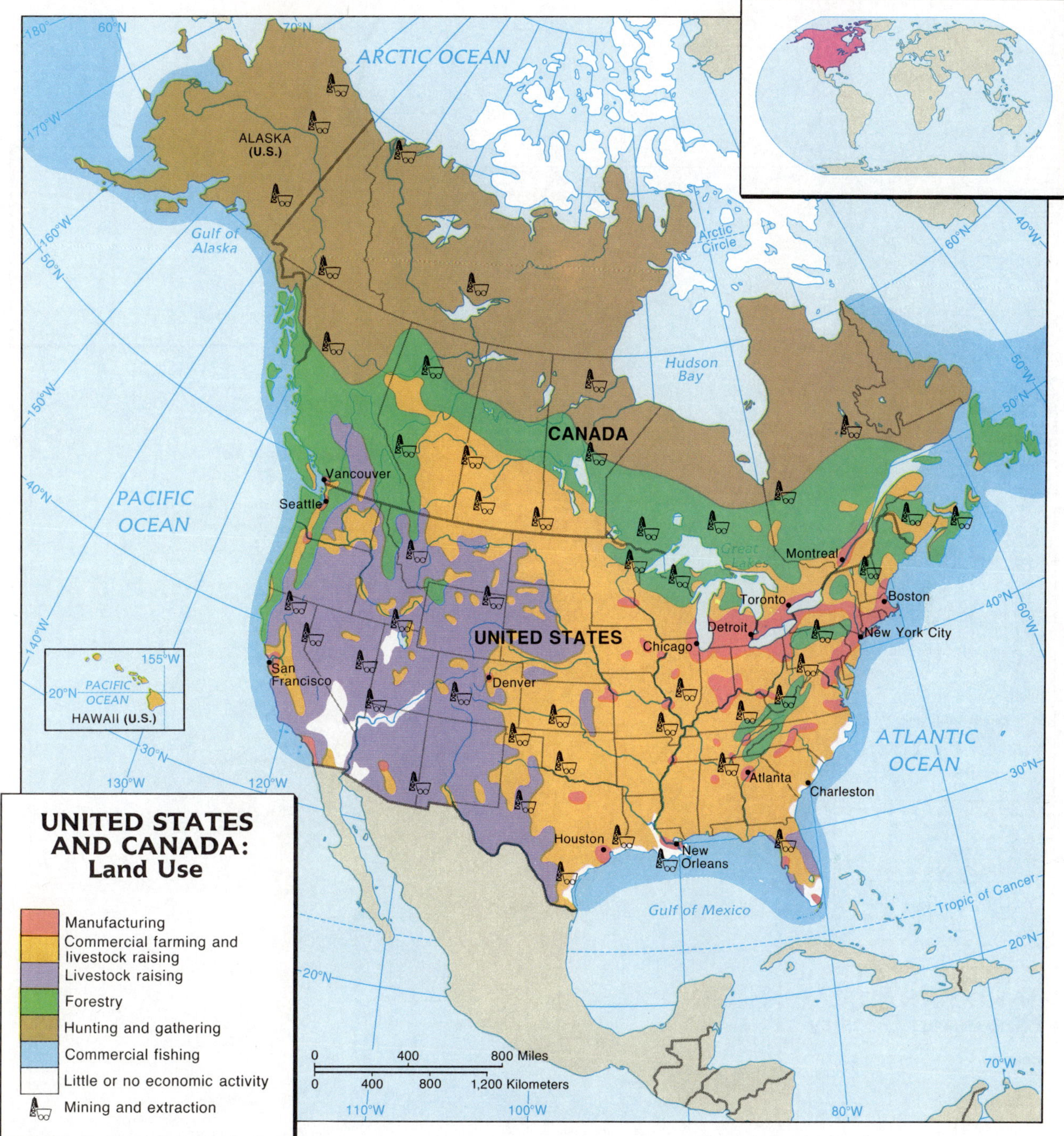
UNITED STATES AND CANADA: Land Use
Manufacturing
Commercial farming and livestock raising
Livestock raising
Forestry
Hunting and gathering
Commercial fishing
Little or no economic activity
Mining and extraction
ARCTIC OCEAN
PACIFIC OCEAN
ATLANTIC OCEAN
Gulf of Alaska
Hudson Bay
Gulf of Mexico
Great Lakes
Arctic Circle
Tropic of Cancer
ALASKA (U.S.)
CANADA
UNITED STATES
HAWAII (U.S.)
Vancouver
Seattle
San Francisco
Denver
Houston
New Orleans
Chicago
Detroit
Toronto
Montreal
Boston
New York City
Atlanta
Charleston
0 400 800 Miles
0 400 800 1,200 Kilometers

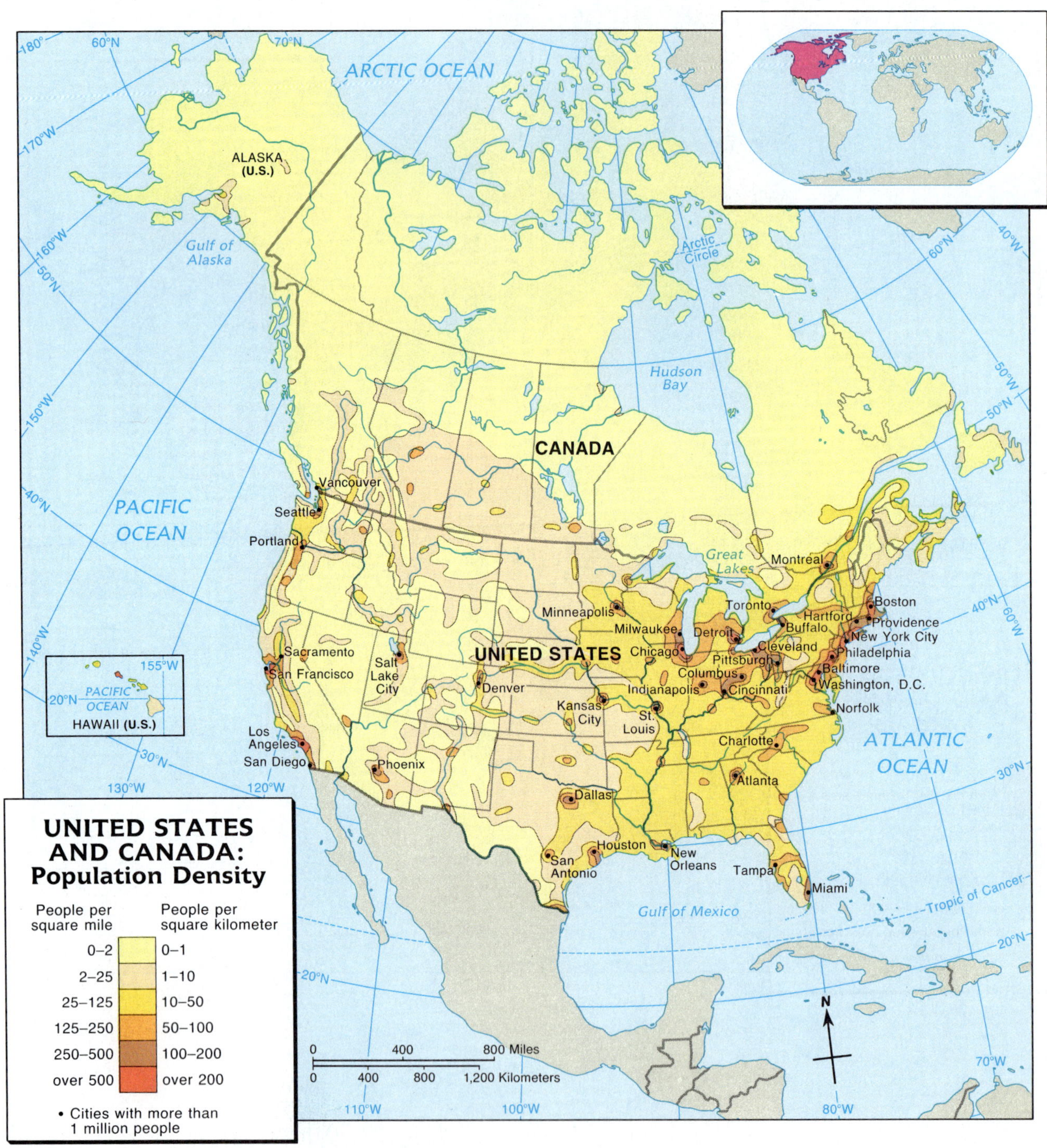
UNITED STATES AND CANADA: Population Density
People per square mile
People per square kilometer
0–2
0–1
2–25
1–10
25–125
10–50
125–250
50–100
250–500
100–200
over 500
over 200
• Cities with more than 1 million people
ARCTIC OCEAN
PACIFIC OCEAN
ATLANTIC OCEAN
Gulf of Alaska
Hudson Bay
Gulf of Mexico
Great Lakes
Arctic Circle
Tropic of Cancer
ALASKA (U.S.)
HAWAII (U.S.)
CANADA
UNITED STATES
Vancouver
Seattle
Portland
Sacramento
San Francisco
Los Angeles
San Diego
Salt Lake City
Phoenix
Denver
Minneapolis
Milwaukee
Chicago
Kansas City
St. Louis
Indianapolis
Dallas
Houston
San Antonio
New Orleans
Detroit
Toronto
Montreal
Buffalo
Cleveland
Pittsburgh
Columbus
Cincinnati
Boston
Hartford
Providence
New York City
Philadelphia
Baltimore
Washington, D.C.
Norfolk
Charlotte
Atlanta
Tampa
Miami
0
400
800 Miles
0
400
800
1,200 Kilometers
N
180°
170°W
160°W
150°W
140°W
130°W
120°W
110°W
100°W
80°W
70°W
60°W
40°W
155°W
60°N
70°N
50°N
40°N
30°N
20°N

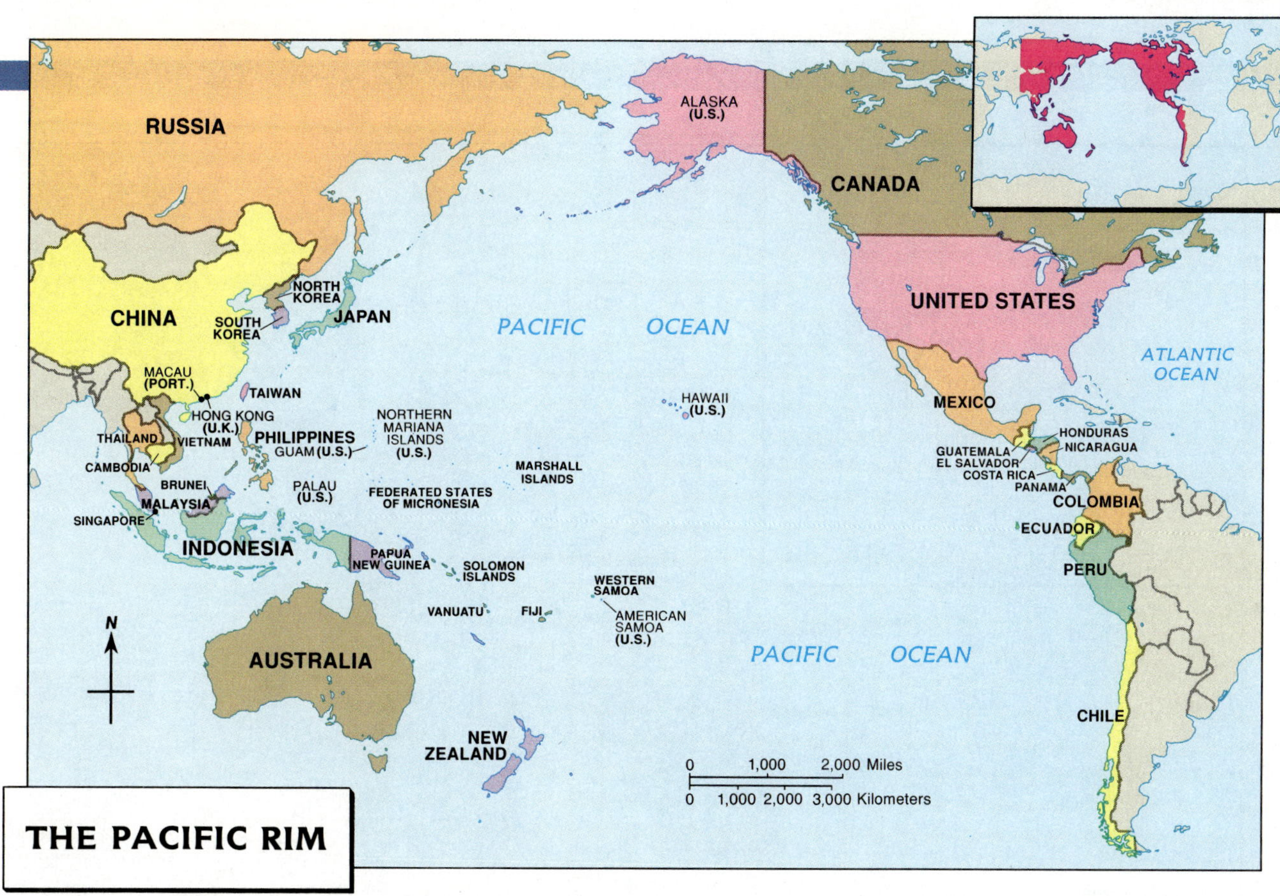

THE PACIFIC RIM

CANADA AND THE UNITED STATES

	Canada	United States
Area	3,851,798 sq mi; 9,976,140 sq km	3,623,420 sq mi; 9,384,658 sq km
Population	26,800,000	252,800,000
People per square mile	7	70
Gross national product	$572 billion	$5,686 billion
Leading exports	Forest products	Machinery and transportation equipment
Most important trading partner	United States	Canada
Capital	Ottawa	Washington, D.C.

RUSSIA
Pt. Barrow
ARCTIC OCEAN
Nome
Fairbanks
AK
CANADA
Anchorage
Valdez
Juneau
Aleutian Islands
PACIFIC OCEAN
0 250 500 Miles
0 250 500 750 Kilometers
PACIFIC OCEAN
WA
OR
ID
MT
WY
CA
NV
UT
CO
AZ
NM
MEXIC
Bellingham
Port Angeles
Seattle
Olympia
Kettle Falls
Spokane
West Glacier
Harlem
Astoria
Ellensburg
Yakima
Vancouver
Portland
Moscow
Walla Walla
Missoula
Great Falls
Wolf Point
Salem
The Dalles
Pendleton
Helena
Newport
Eugene
Butte
Forsyth
Coos Bay
Bend
New Meadows
Bozeman
Billings
Buffalo
Roseburg
Burns
Yellowstone
Grants Pass
Boise
Arco
Gillette
Crescent City
Klamath Falls
Rapid City
Yreka
Lakeview
Pocatello
Shoshoni
Eureka
Twin Falls
Casper
Redding
Winnemucca
Great Salt Lake
Wells
Ft. Laram
Rock Springs
Reno
Cheyenne
Carson City
Salt Lake City
Provo
Vernal
Steamboat Springs
Sacramento
San Francisco
Ely
Delta
Denver
San Jose
Tonopah
Milford
Thompson
Grand Jct.
Burlingto
Colorado Spri
Alamo
Pueblo
St. George
Lamar
Durango
Las Vegas
Grand Canyon Village
Tuba City
Kingman
Santa Barbara
Flagstaff
Gallup
Santa Fe
Needles
Los Angeles
San Bernardino
Albuquerque
Amar
Tucumcari
Phoenix
San Diego
Yuma
Roswell
Lubboc
Tucson
Lordsburg
Las Cruces
Carlsbad
El Paso
Nogales
Odessa
Kauai
Oahu
Honolulu
Molokai
Maui
PACIFIC OCEAN
HI
Hawaii
Kailua-Kona
Hilo
0 100 Miles
0 100 Kilometers

CANADA
ATLANTIC OCEAN
Gulf of Mexico
CUBA
Lake Superior
Lake Michigan
Lake Huron
Lake Ontario
Lake Erie
UNITED STATES: Road Map
Interstate highway
Other federal highway
State highway
National capital
State capital
Other city
0 100 200 300 Miles
0 100 200 300 400 Kilometers

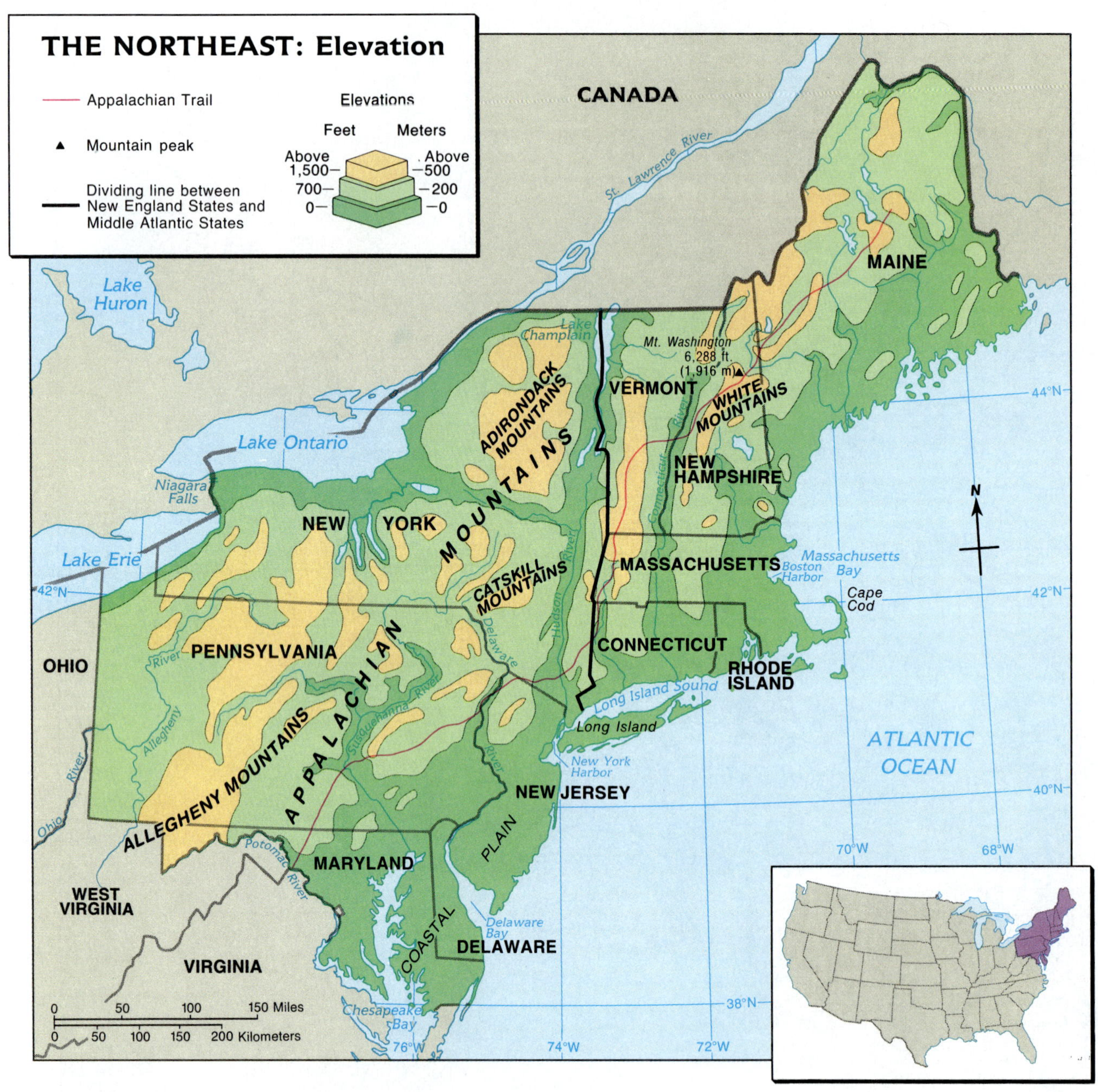
THE NORTHEAST: Elevation
Appalachian Trail
Mountain peak
Dividing line between New England States and Middle Atlantic States
Elevations
Feet
Meters
Above 1,500
700
0
Above 500
200
0
CANADA
St. Lawrence River
Lake Huron
Lake Ontario
Niagara Falls
Lake Erie
Lake Champlain
MAINE
Mt. Washington 6,288 ft. (1,916 m)
VERMONT
WHITE MOUNTAINS
ADIRONDACK MOUNTAINS
NEW HAMPSHIRE
NEW YORK
MOUNTAINS
CATSKILL MOUNTAINS
MASSACHUSETTS
Massachusetts Bay
Boston Harbor
Cape Cod
CONNECTICUT
RHODE ISLAND
Long Island Sound
Long Island
New York Harbor
ATLANTIC OCEAN
OHIO
PENNSYLVANIA
APPALACHIAN
ALLEGHENY MOUNTAINS
Allegheny River
Ohio River
Susquehanna River
Delaware River
Hudson River
Connecticut River
Potomac River
NEW JERSEY
COASTAL PLAIN
MARYLAND
DELAWARE
Delaware Bay
Chesapeake Bay
WEST VIRGINIA
VIRGINIA
0 50 100 150 Miles
0 50 100 150 200 Kilometers
44°N
42°N
40°N
38°N
76°W
74°W
72°W
70°W
68°W
N

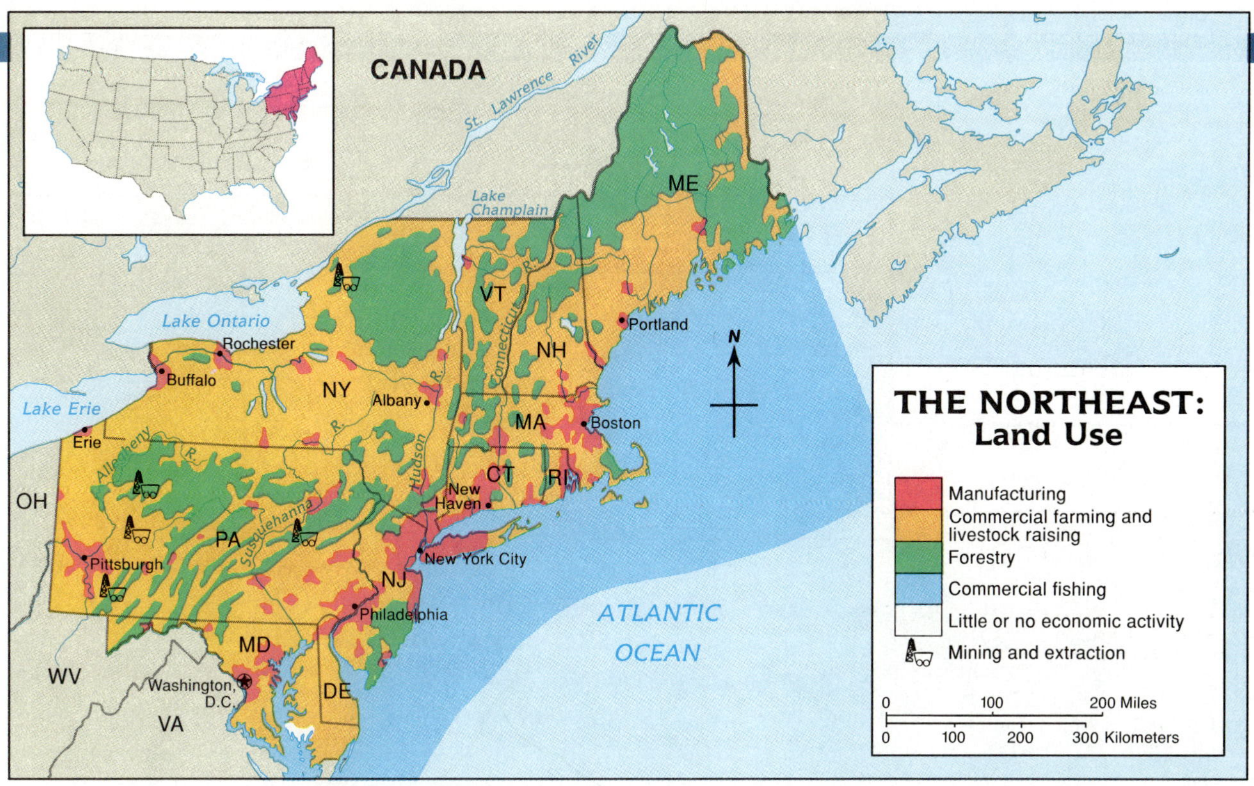

STATES OF THE NORTHEAST

State	Capital	Population	Area in sq mi (sq km)	Date of Statehood
Connecticut	Hartford	3,287,116	5,544 (14,358)	1788
Delaware	Dover	666,168	2,489 (6,446)	1787
Maine	Augusta	1,227,928	35,387 (91,652)	1820
Maryland	Annapolis	4,781,468	12,407 (32,134)	1788
Massachusetts	Boston	6,016,425	10,555 (27,337)	1788
New Hampshire	Concord	1,109,252	9,351 (24,219)	1788
New Jersey	Trenton	7,730,188	8,722 (22,590)	1787
New York	Albany	17,990,455	54,475 (141,090)	1788
Pennsylvania	Harrisburg	11,881,643	46,058 (119,290)	1787
Rhode Island	Providence	1,003,464	1,545 (4,002)	1790
Vermont	Montpelier	562,758	9,615 (24,903)	1791

Population figures: 1990 Census

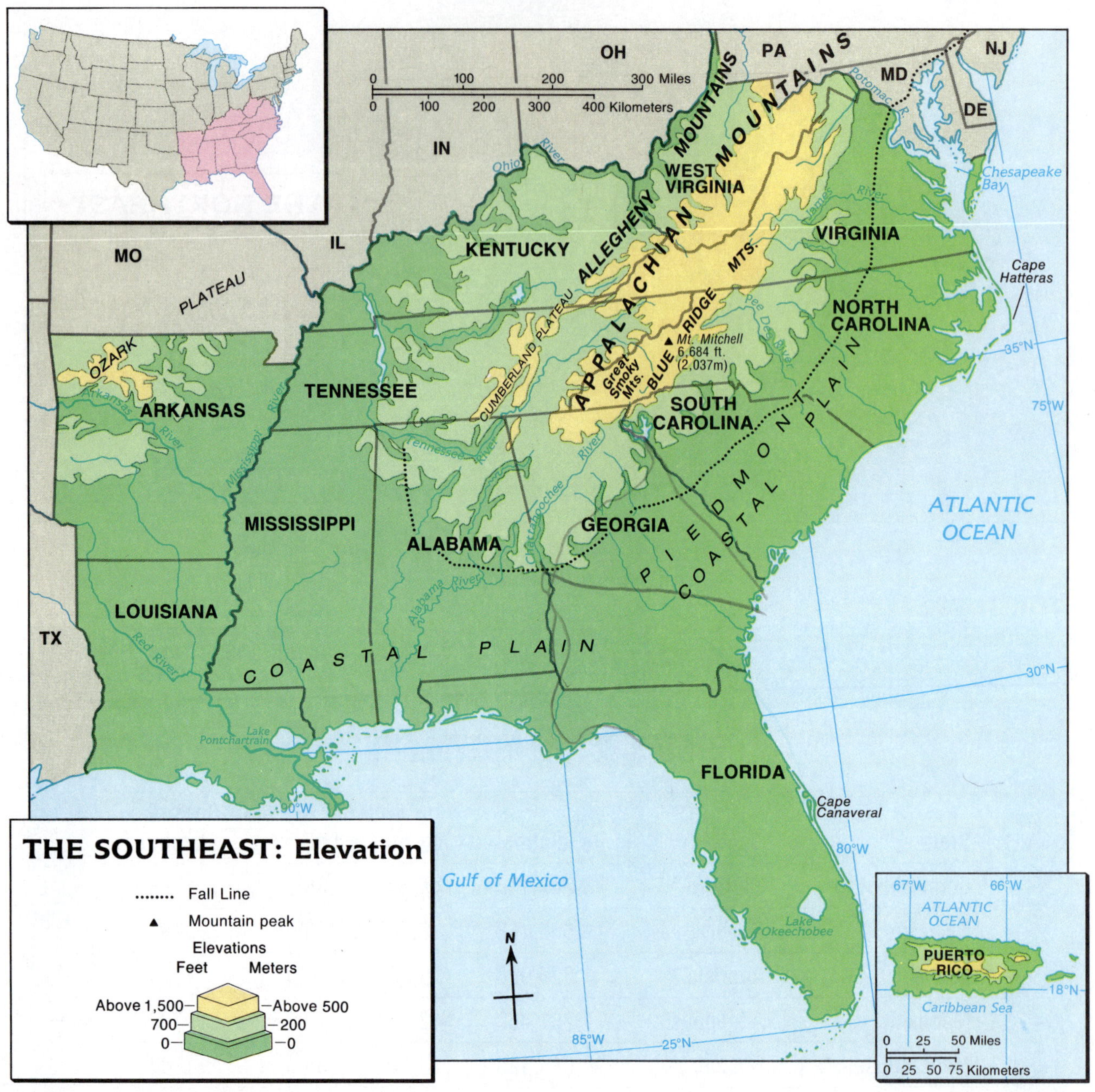
THE SOUTHEAST: Elevation
Fall Line
Mountain peak
Elevations
Feet
Meters
Above 1,500
700
0
Above 500
200
0
0 100 200 300 Miles
0 100 200 300 400 Kilometers
OH
PA
NJ
MD
DE
IN
IL
MO
TX
KENTUCKY
WEST VIRGINIA
VIRGINIA
NORTH CAROLINA
SOUTH CAROLINA
TENNESSEE
ARKANSAS
MISSISSIPPI
ALABAMA
GEORGIA
LOUISIANA
FLORIDA
APPALACHIAN MOUNTAINS
ALLEGHENY MOUNTAINS
BLUE RIDGE MTS.
CUMBERLAND PLATEAU
Great Smoky Mts.
Mt. Mitchell 6,684 ft. (2,037m)
OZARK PLATEAU
PIEDMONT
COASTAL PLAIN
Ohio River
Potomac
James River
Pee Dee River
Tennessee River
Mississippi River
Arkansas River
Red River
Alabama River
Chattahoochee River
Lake Pontchartrain
Lake Okeechobee
Chesapeake Bay
Cape Hatteras
Cape Canaveral
ATLANTIC OCEAN
Gulf of Mexico
35°N
30°N
25°N
75°W
80°W
85°W
90°W
N
PUERTO RICO
ATLANTIC OCEAN
Caribbean Sea
67°W
66°W
18°N
0 25 50 Miles
0 25 50 75 Kilometers

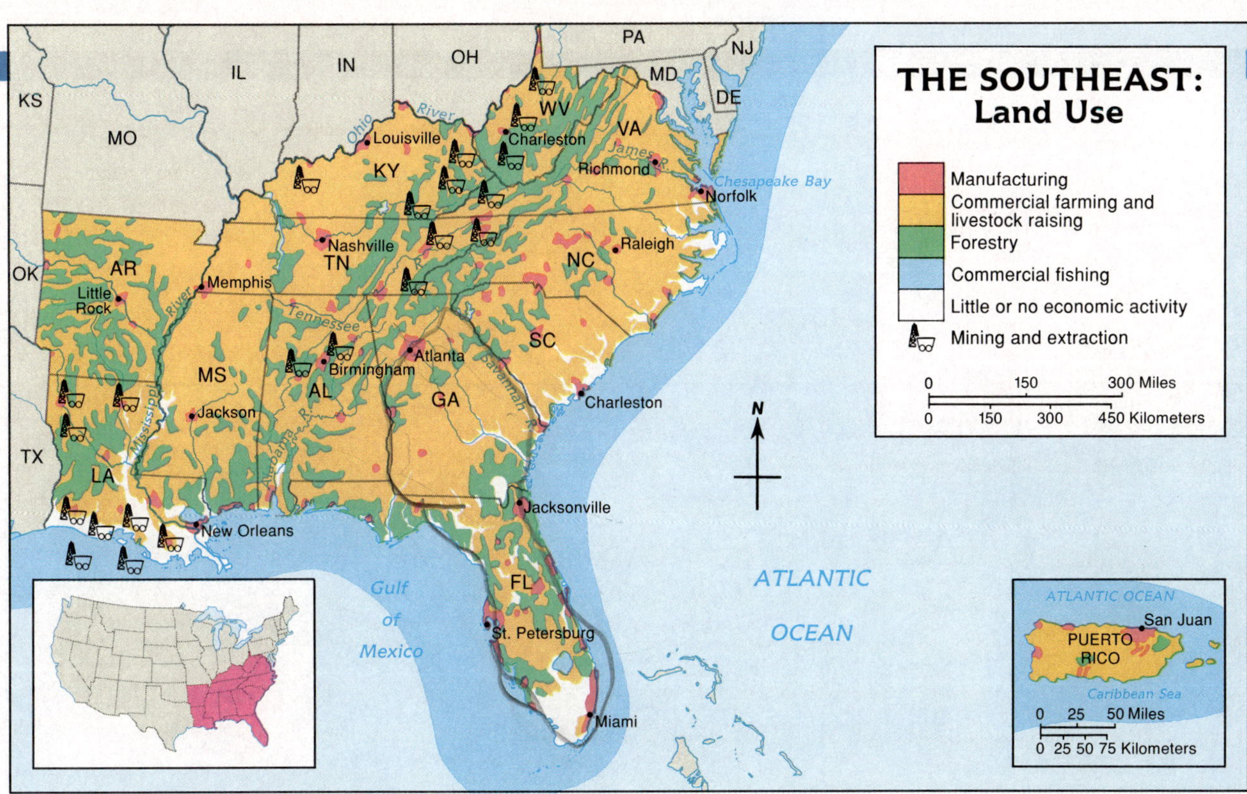

STATES OF THE SOUTHEAST

State	Capital	Population	Area in sq mi (sq km)	Date of Statehood
Alabama	Montgomery	4,040,587	52,423 (135,776)	1819
Arkansas	Little Rock	2,350,725	53,182 (137,741)	1836
Florida	Tallahassee	12,937,926	65,758 (170,314)	1845
Georgia	Atlanta	6,478,216	59,441 (153,952)	1788
Kentucky	Frankfort	3,685,296	40,411 (104,664)	1792
Louisiana	Baton Rouge	4,219,000	51,843 (134,273)	1812
Mississippi	Jackson	2,573,216	48,434 (125,444)	1817
North Carolina	Raleigh	6,628,637	53,821 (139,396)	1789
South Carolina	Columbia	3,486,703	32,007 (82,898)	1788
Tennessee	Nashville	4,877,185	42,146 (109,158)	1796
Virginia	Richmond	6,187,358	42,769 (110,772)	1788
West Virginia	Charleston	1,793,477	24,231 (65,758)	1863

Population figures: 1990 Census

THE MIDDLE WEST: Elevation
Elevations
Feet
Meters
Above 1,500
Above 500
700
200
0
0
Mountain peak
Dividing line between Great Lakes States and Plains States
0 100 200 300 Miles
0 100 200 300 400 Kilometers
CANADA
MT
WY
COLORADO
NM
TEXAS
OKLAHOMA
ARKANSAS
MS
TENNESSEE
KENTUCKY
NC
VIRGINIA
WEST VIRGINIA
PA
NORTH DAKOTA
SOUTH DAKOTA
NEBRASKA
KANSAS
MINNESOTA
IOWA
MISSOURI
WISCONSIN
ILLINOIS
INDIANA
OHIO
MICHIGAN
GREAT PLAINS
INTERIOR PLAINS
CENTRAL PLAINS
OZARK PLATEAU
BLACK HILLS
Harney Peak 7,242 ft. (2,207 m)
MESABI RANGE
Lake of the Woods
Lake Sakakawea
Lake Oahe
Lake Superior
Lake Michigan
Lake Huron
Lake Erie
Lake Ontario
Missouri River
Platte River
Arkansas River
Des Moines River
Mississippi River
Wisconsin River
Illinois River
Wabash River
Ohio River
N

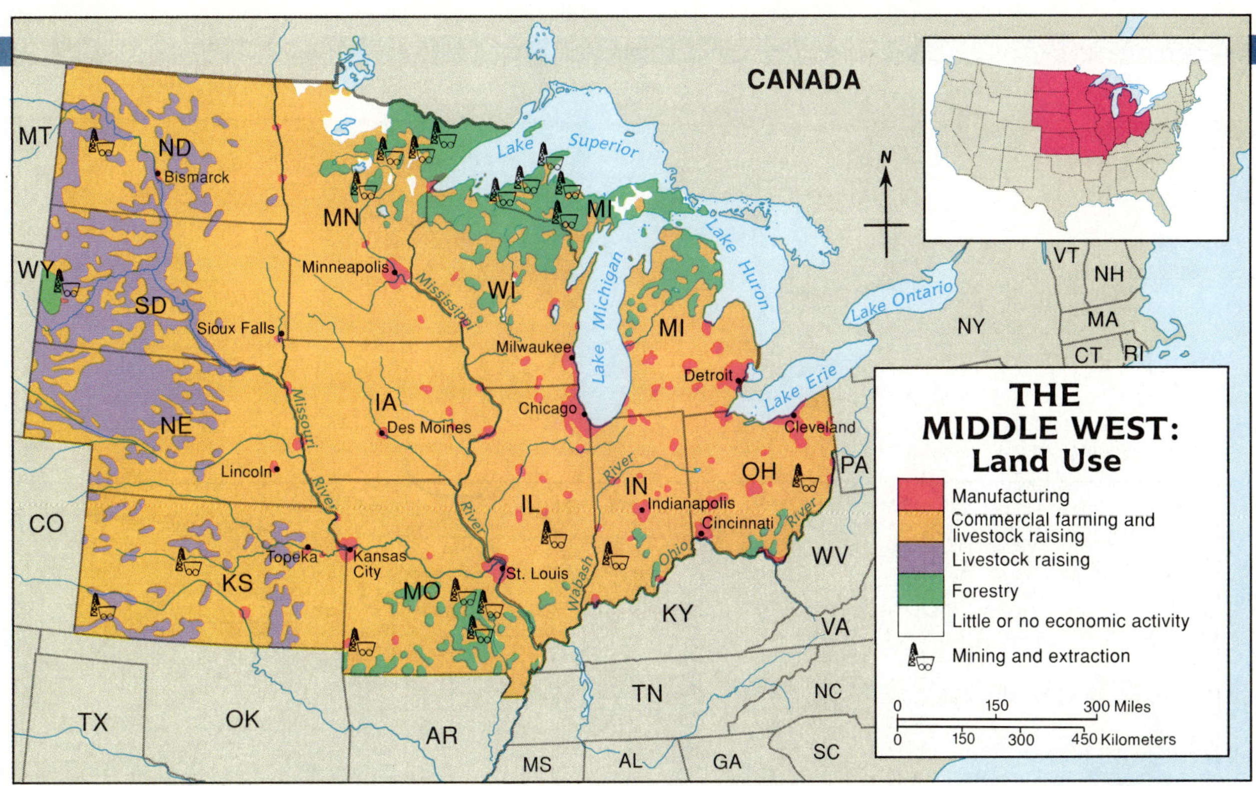

STATES OF THE MIDDLE WEST

State	Capital	Population	Area in sq mi (sq km)	Date of Statehood
Illinois	Springfield	11,430,602	57,918 (150,008)	1818
Indiana	Indianapolis	5,544,159	36,420 (94,328)	1816
Iowa	Des Moines	2,776,755	56,276 (145,755)	1846
Kansas	Topeka	2,477,574	82,282 (213,110)	1861
Michigan	Lansing	9,295,297	96,810 (250,738)	1837
Minnesota	St. Paul	4,375,099	86,943 (225,182)	1858
Missouri	Jefferson City	5,117,073	69,709 (180,546)	1821
Nebraska	Lincoln	1,578,385	77,358 (200,357)	1867
North Dakota	Bismarck	638,800	70,704 (183,123)	1889
Ohio	Columbus	10,847,115	44,828 (116,105)	1803
South Dakota	Pierre	696,004	77,121 (199,743)	1889
Wisconsin	Madison	4,891,769	65,503 (169,653)	1848

Population figures: 1990 Census

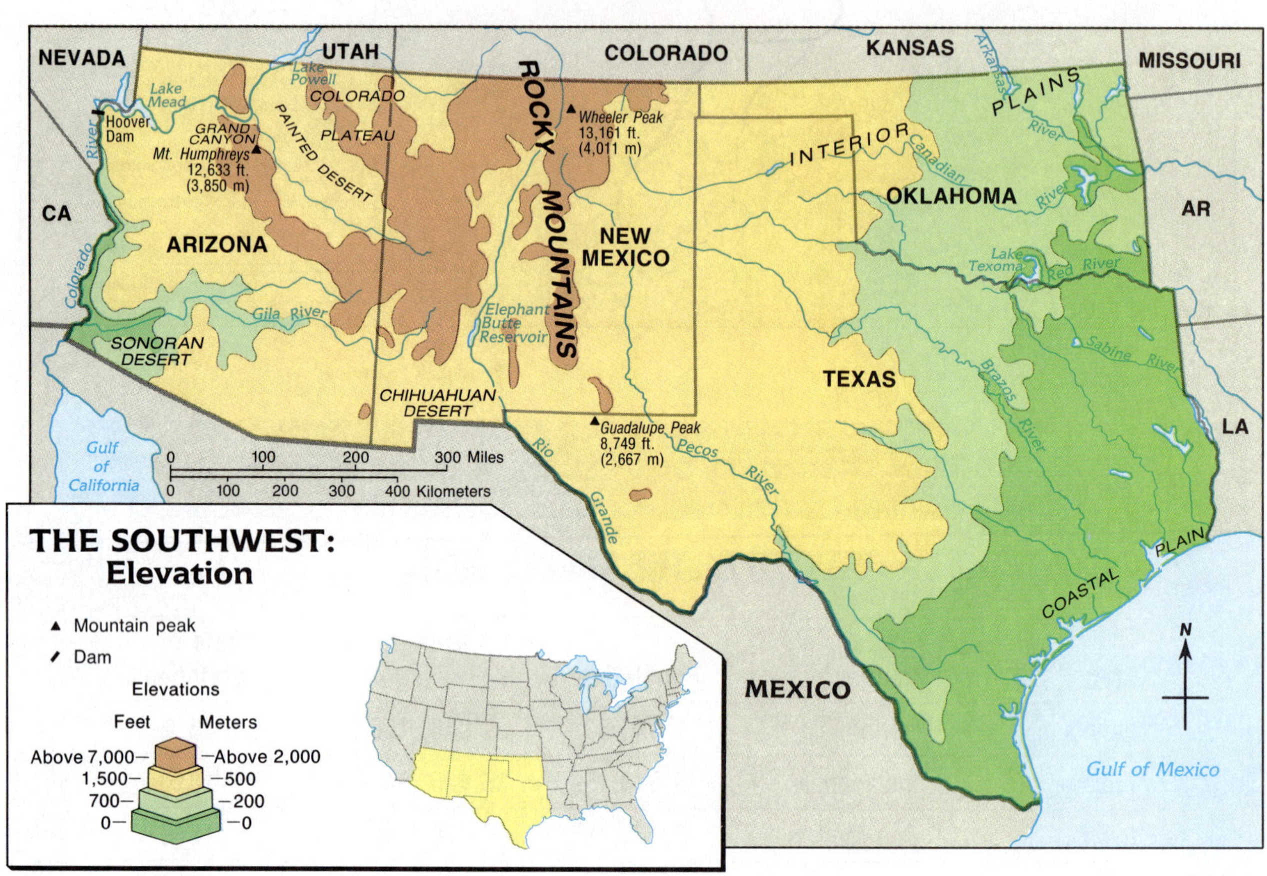
NEVADA
UTAH
COLORADO
KANSAS
MISSOURI
Lake Mead
Lake Powell
COLORADO PLATEAU
ROCKY MOUNTAINS
Wheeler Peak 13,161 ft. (4,011 m)
Hoover Dam
GRAND CANYON
Mt. Humphreys 12,633 ft. (3,850 m)
PAINTED DESERT
INTERIOR PLAINS
Arkansas River
Canadian River
OKLAHOMA
CA
AR
ARIZONA
NEW MEXICO
Lake Texoma
Red River
Colorado River
Gila River
Elephant Butte Reservoir
SONORAN DESERT
TEXAS
Sabine River
Brazos River
CHIHUAHUAN DESERT
Guadalupe Peak 8,749 ft. (2,667 m)
LA
Gulf of California
0 100 200 300 Miles
0 100 200 300 400 Kilometers
Pecos River
Rio Grande
COASTAL PLAIN
THE SOUTHWEST: Elevation
Mountain peak
Dam
Elevations
Feet Meters
Above 7,000— —Above 2,000
1,500— —500
700— —200
0— —0
MEXICO
N
Gulf of Mexico

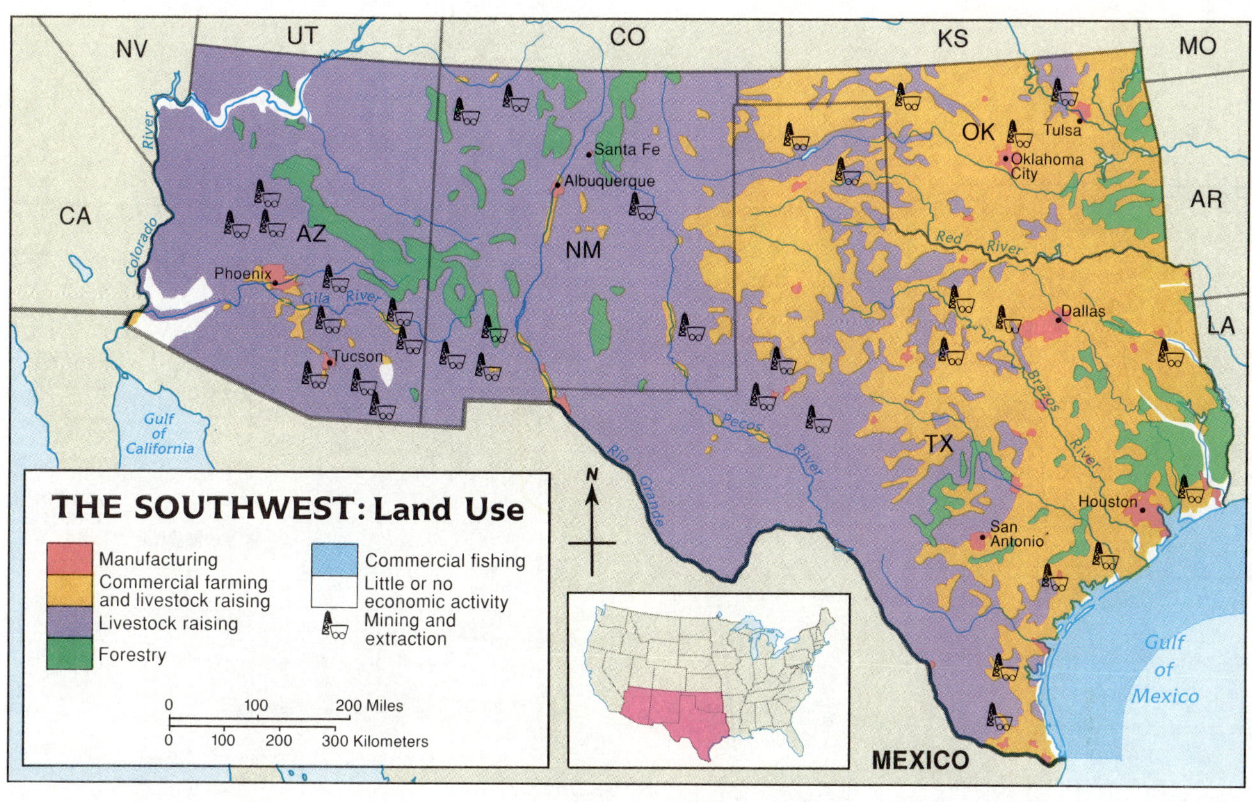

STATES OF THE SOUTHWEST

State	Capital	Population	Area in sq mi (sq km)	Date of Statehood
Arizona	Phoenix	3,665,228	114,006 (295,276)	1912
New Mexico	Santa Fe	1,515,069	121,598 (314,938)	1912
Oklahoma	Oklahoma City	3,145,585	69,903 (181,049)	1907
Texas	Austin	16,986,510	268,601 (695,677)	1845

Population figures: 1990 Census

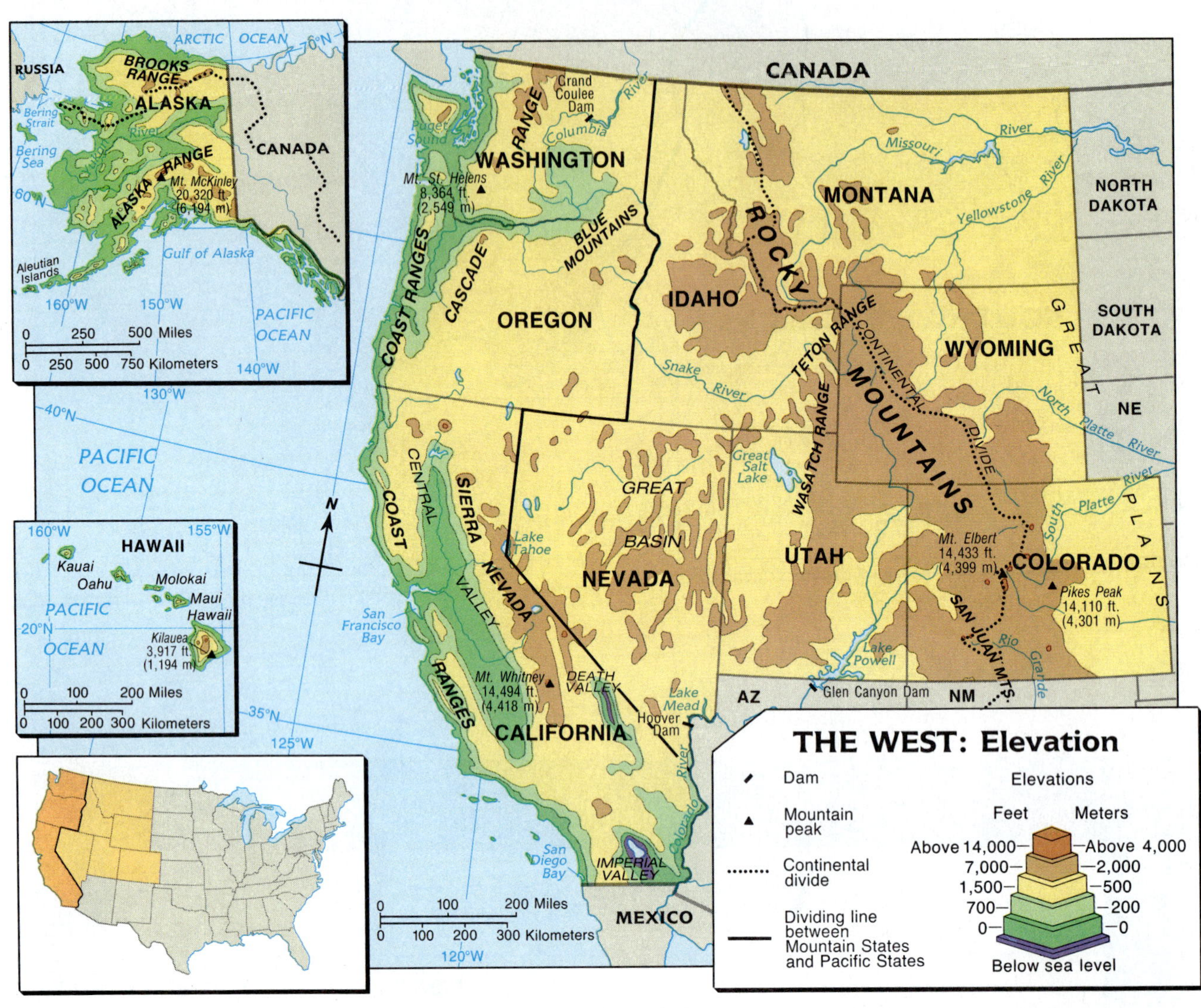
THE WEST: Elevation
CANADA
WASHINGTON
MONTANA
NORTH DAKOTA
SOUTH DAKOTA
IDAHO
OREGON
WYOMING
NE
NEVADA
UTAH
COLORADO
CALIFORNIA
AZ
NM
MEXICO
PACIFIC OCEAN
ROCKY MOUNTAINS
GREAT PLAINS
GREAT BASIN
CASCADE RANGE
COAST RANGES
BLUE MOUNTAINS
TETON RANGE
WASATCH RANGE
CONTINENTAL DIVIDE
SAN JUAN MTS.
SIERRA NEVADA
CENTRAL VALLEY
COAST RANGES
DEATH VALLEY
IMPERIAL VALLEY
Grand Coulee Dam
Columbia River
Puget Sound
Mt. St. Helens 8,364 ft. (2,549 m)
Missouri River
Yellowstone River
Snake River
North Platte River
South Platte River
Great Salt Lake
Lake Tahoe
San Francisco Bay
Mt. Whitney 14,494 ft. (4,418 m)
Lake Mead
Hoover Dam
Colorado River
San Diego Bay
Lake Powell
Glen Canyon Dam
Rio Grande
Mt. Elbert 14,433 ft. (4,399 m)
Pikes Peak 14,110 ft. (4,301 m)
40°N
35°N
130°W
125°W
120°W
N
0 100 200 Miles
0 100 200 300 Kilometers
RUSSIA
ARCTIC OCEAN
BROOKS RANGE
ALASKA
CANADA
Bering Strait
Bering Sea
ALASKA RANGE
Mt. McKinley 20,320 ft. (6,194 m)
60°N
Aleutian Islands
Gulf of Alaska
160°W
150°W
140°W
PACIFIC OCEAN
0 250 500 Miles
0 250 500 750 Kilometers
HAWAII
160°W
155°W
Kauai
Oahu
Molokai
Maui
Hawaii
PACIFIC OCEAN
20°N
Kilauea 3,917 ft. (1,194 m)
0 100 200 Miles
0 100 200 300 Kilometers
Dam
Mountain peak
Continental divide
Dividing line between Mountain States and Pacific States
Elevations
Feet
Meters
Above 14,000
7,000
1,500
700
0
Above 4,000
2,000
500
200
0
Below sea level

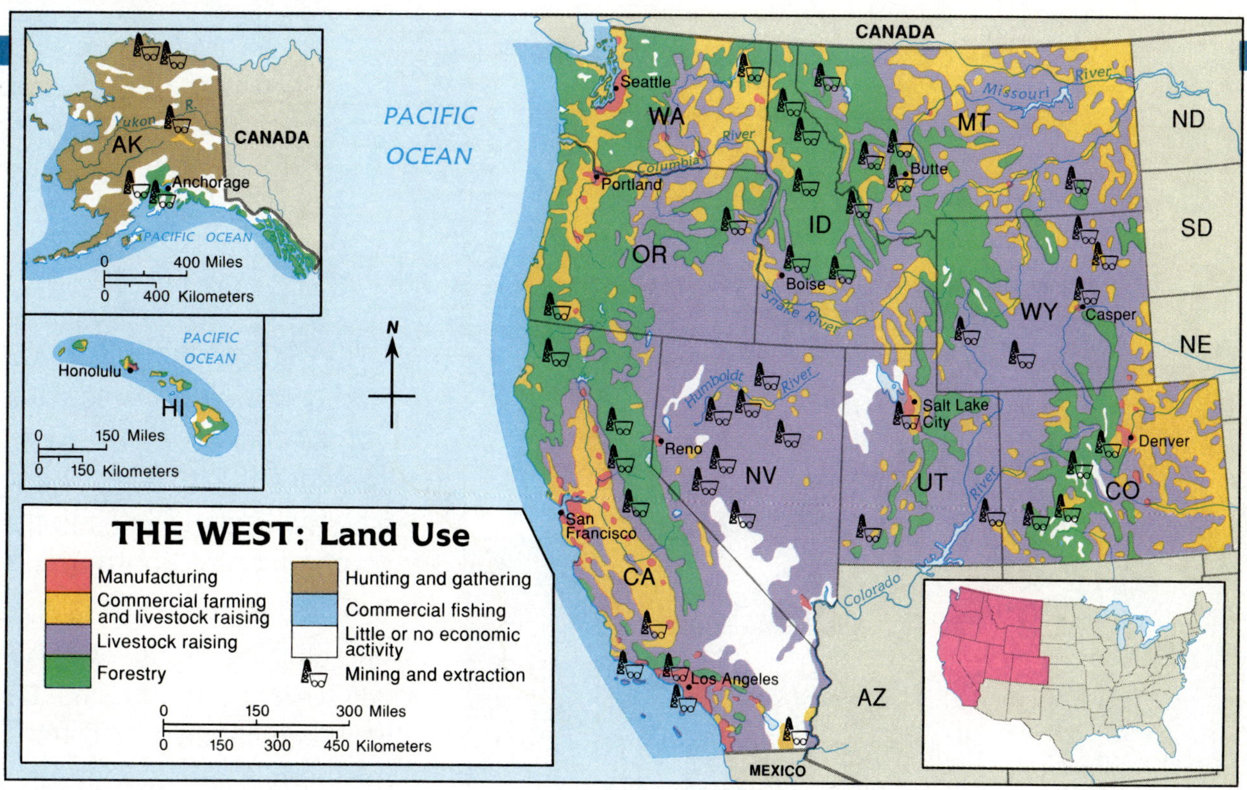

STATES OF THE WEST

State	Capital	Population	Area in sq mi (sq km)	Date of Statehood
Alaska	Juneau	550,043	656,424 (1,700,138)	1959
California	Sacramento	29,760,021	163,707 (424,001)	1850
Colorado	Denver	3,294,394	104,100 (269,619)	1876
Hawaii	Honolulu	1,108,229	10,392 (28,313)	1959
Idaho	Boise	1,006,749	83,574 (216,457)	1890
Montana	Helena	799,065	147,046 (380,849)	1889
Nevada	Carson City	1,201,833	110,567 (286,369)	1864
Oregon	Salem	2,842,321	98,386 (254,820)	1859
Utah	Salt Lake City	1,722,850	84,904 (219,901)	1896
Washington	Olympia	4,866,692	71,303 (184,675)	1889
Wyoming	Cheyenne	453,588	97,818 (253,349)	1890

Population figures: 1990 Census

LATIN AMERICA

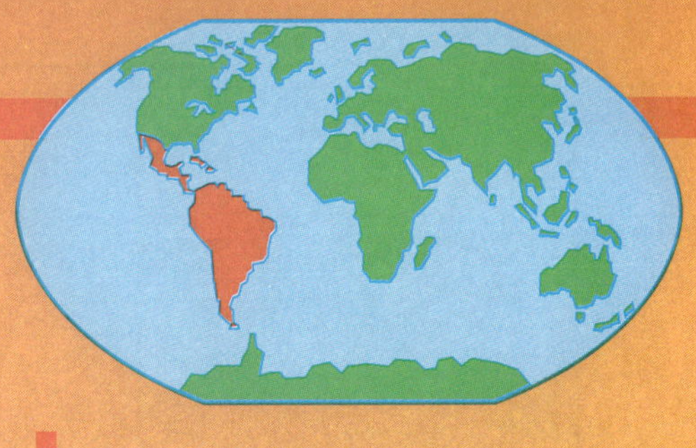

Latin America straddles two continents, North America and South America. This vast region stretches from Mexico's border with the United States to the southern tip of South America, and also includes the islands of the Caribbean Sea. Latin America has towering mountains, tropical islands, windswept plains, and the world's largest rain forest. It also houses some of the largest urban areas in the world, including the world's largest city—Mexico City.

Latin America gets its name from Latin, an old language that

Lifestyles vary greatly in Latin America. Some people live and work in cities. Others live off the land.

BRAZIL

Brazil is larger than the 48 states of the continental United States.

This Aztec temple in Mexico and the Incan vase from Peru are part of Latin America's past.

was the "grandparent" of many languages spoken in Europe. For hundreds of years Latin America was ruled by European countries. Foreign rule greatly affected life in this region. One result is that most of the people in Latin America today speak the "Latin" languages called Spanish and Portuguese.

Two landforms greatly shape life in Latin America—the Andes Mountains and the Amazon River. As you look at the maps in this section, hunt for clues that show how these landforms affect the climate, land use, and settlement of the land around them.

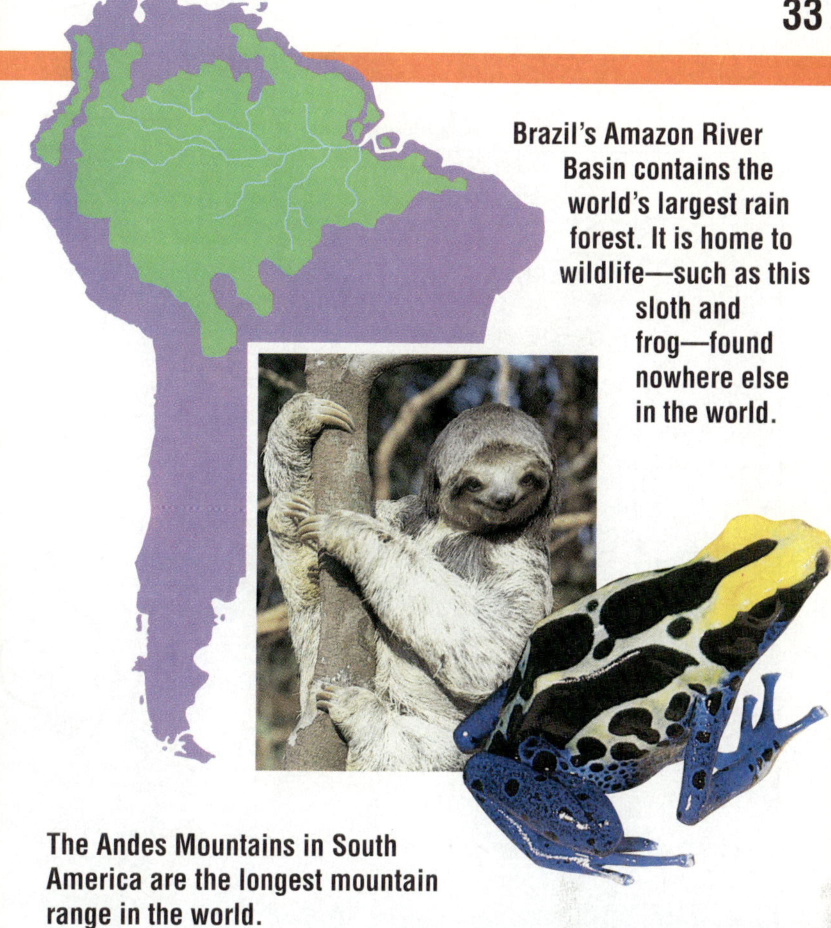

Brazil's Amazon River Basin contains the world's largest rain forest. It is home to wildlife—such as this sloth and frog—found nowhere else in the world.

The Andes Mountains in South America are the longest mountain range in the world.

Latin America contains two of the world's largest urban areas, including São Paulo, Brazil (*below*). According to the graph, what is the world's largest urban area?

WORLD'S LARGEST URBAN AREAS

Population (in millions): 0, 5, 10, 15, 20

Mexico City Tokyo São Paulo New York

Soccer is the most popular sport in Latin America.

LATIN AMERICA
Physical
0 400 800 Miles
0 400 800 1,200 Kilometers
NORTH AMERICA
SIERRA MADRE OCCIDENTAL
SIERRA MADRE ORIENTAL
Baja California
Gulf of California
Gulf of Mexico
Tropic of Cancer
Cuba
Greater Antilles
Hispaniola
Yucatán Peninsula
Caribbean Sea
Lesser Antilles
CENTRAL AMERICA
Lake Nicaragua
Isthmus of Panama
Gulf of Panama
Guajira Peninsula
Lake Maracaibo
Orinoco R.
LLANOS
GUIANA HIGHLANDS
Cauca River
Magdalena R.
Equator
Galápagos Islands
Gulf of Guayaquil
Aguja Point
PACIFIC OCEAN
ANDES MOUNTAINS
Japurá
Rio Negro
AMAZON BASIN
Amazon River
Marajó Island
Cape São Roque
Marañon R.
Ucayali River
Purus River
Madeira R.
Tapajós R.
Xingu River
Tocantins River
Parnaíba River
São Francisco River
SOUTH AMERICA
MATO GROSSO PLATEAU
Araguaia
Lake Titicaca
Lake Poopó
BRAZILIAN HIGHLANDS
Paraguay R.
Pilcomayo River
GRAN CHACO
Tropic of Capricorn
ATACAMA DESERT
ANDES MOUNTAINS
Salado River
Paraná River
Uruguay
Mt. Aconcagua 22,834 ft. (6,960 m)
PAMPAS
Rio de la Plata
ATLANTIC OCEAN
Blanca Bay
San Matías Gulf
Chiloé Island
PATAGONIA
Gulf of San Jorge
Strait of Magellan
Falkland Islands
Tierra del Fuego
Cape Horn
South Georgia
N
75°W
60°W
45°W
105°W
90°W
30°N
15°N
0°
15°S
30°S
45°S

LATIN AMERICA
Political
National capital
Other city
0 400 800 Miles
0 400 800 1,200 Kilometers
UNITED STATES
MEXICO
Monterrey
Guadalajara
Mexico City
Gulf of California
Rio Grande
Gulf of Mexico
BAHAMAS
Havana
CUBA
TURKS AND CAICOS ISLANDS (U.K.)
HAITI
PUERTO RICO (U.S.)
San Juan
VIRGIN ISLANDS (U.K.)
VIRGIN ISLANDS (U.S.)
ST KITTS AND NEVIS
ANTIGUA AND BARBUDA
GUADELOUPE (FR.)
DOMINICA
MARTINIQUE (FR.)
BARBADOS
ST. LUCIA
GRENADA
ST. VINCENT AND THE GRENADINES
TRINIDAD AND TOBAGO
Port-au-Prince
JAMAICA
Kingston
Santo Domingo
DOMINICAN REPUBLIC
Caribbean Sea
BELIZE
Belmopan
GUATEMALA
HONDURAS
Guatemala City
Tegucigalpa
San Salvador
EL SALVADOR
NICARAGUA
Managua
NETHERLANDS ANTILLES (NETH.)
ARUBA (NETH.)
Barranquilla
San José
COSTA RICA
Panama City
PANAMA
Maracaibo
Valencia
Caracas
Lake Maracaibo
Orinoco R.
VENEZUELA
Georgetown
Paramaribo
Cayenne
GUYANA
SURINAME
FRENCH GUIANA (FR.)
Medellín
Bogotá
Cali
Magdalena R.
COLOMBIA
Equator
GALÁPAGOS ISLANDS (ECUADOR)
ECUADOR
Quito
Guayaquil
Iquitos
Manaus
Amazon River
Belém
PACIFIC
OCEAN
PERU
Trujillo
Callao
Lima
Cuzco
Recife
São Francisco River
BRAZIL
Salvador (Bahia)
Lake Titicaca
Arequipa
La Paz
BOLIVIA
Sucre
Brasília
Paraguay R.
Belo Horizonte
Tropic of Capricorn
Tropic of Cancer
Antofagasta
Tucumán
PARAGUAY
River
Rio de Janeiro
São Paulo
Asunción
Paraná River
Uruguay
CHILE
Pôrto Alegre
Córdoba
Rosario
URUGUAY
Valparaíso
Santiago
Buenos Aires
Montevideo
Río de la Plata
ATLANTIC
OCEAN
Concepción
ARGENTINA
Punta Arenas
Strait of Magellan
FALKLAND ISLANDS (U.K.)
SOUTH GEORGIA (U.K.)
N
105°W
90°W
75°W
60°W
45°W
30°N
15°N
0°
15°S
30°S
45°S

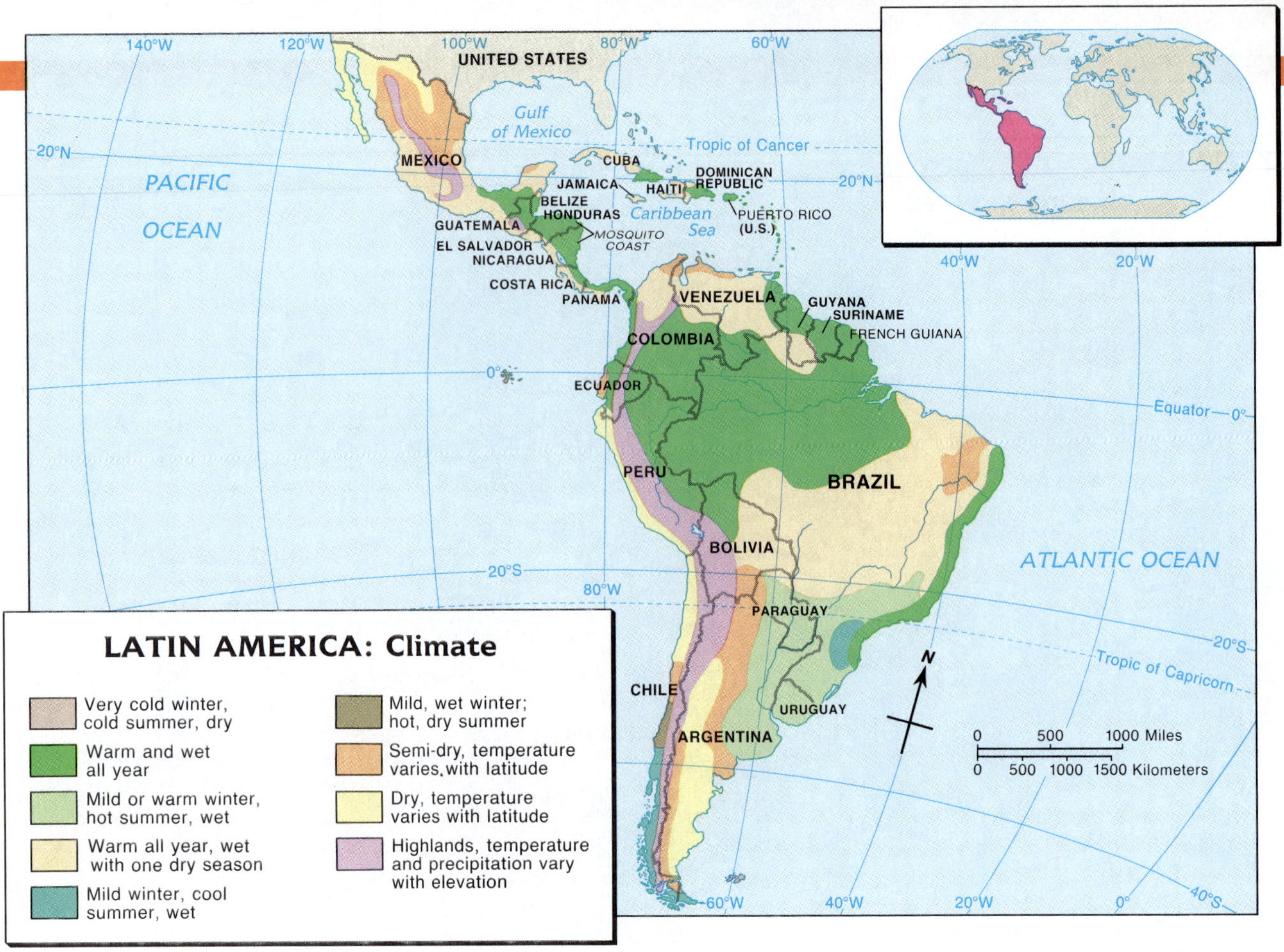

LATIN AMERICA: Climate

- Very cold winter, cold summer, dry
- Warm and wet all year
- Mild or warm winter, hot summer, wet
- Warm all year, wet with one dry season
- Mild winter, cool summer, wet
- Mild, wet winter; hot, dry summer
- Semi-dry, temperature varies with latitude
- Dry, temperature varies with latitude
- Highlands, temperature and precipitation vary with elevation

0 500 1000 Miles

0 500 1000 1500 Kilometers

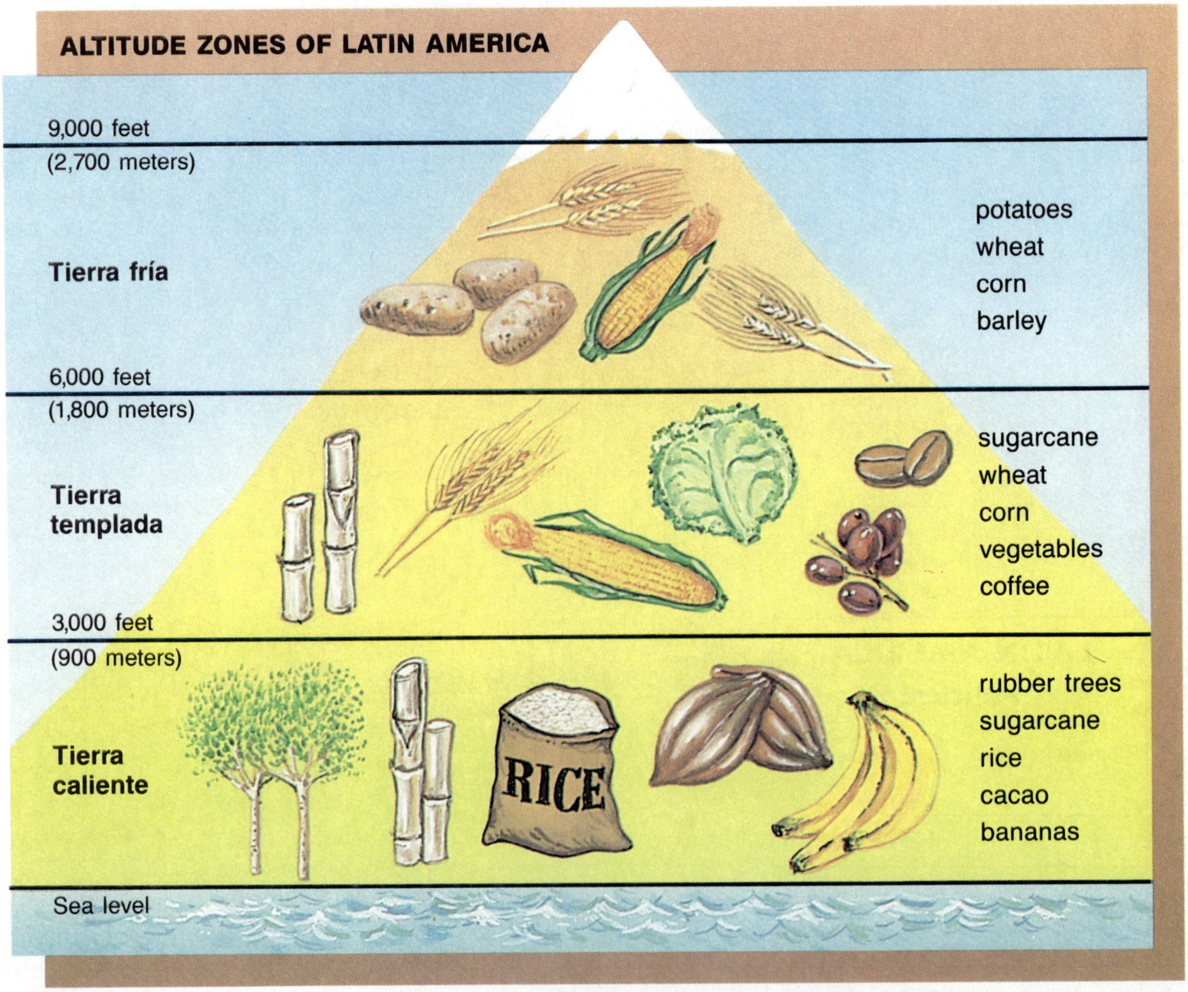

ALTITUDE ZONES OF LATIN AMERICA

9,000 feet (2,700 meters)

Tierra fría

potatoes
wheat
corn
barley

6,000 feet (1,800 meters)

Tierra templada

sugarcane
wheat
corn
vegetables
coffee

3,000 feet (900 meters)

Tierra caliente

rubber trees
sugarcane
rice
cacao
bananas

RICE

Sea level

LATIN AMERICA: Land Use
Manufacturing
Commercial farming and livestock raising
Livestock raising
Subsistence farming
Forestry with farming, hunting, and gathering
Commercial fishing
Little or no economic activity
Mining and extraction
Tourism
UNITED STATES
Gulf of Mexico
Tropic of Cancer
PACIFIC OCEAN
ATLANTIC OCEAN
Caribbean Sea
MEXICO
CUBA
JAMAICA
HAITI
DOMINICAN REPUBLIC
PUERTO RICO (U.S.)
BELIZE
GUATEMALA
HONDURAS
EL SALVADOR
NICARAGUA
COSTA RICA
PANAMA
GUYANA
SURINAME
FRENCH GUIANA
VENEZUELA
COLOMBIA
ECUADOR
PERU
BRAZIL
BOLIVIA
PARAGUAY
CHILE
URUGUAY
ARGENTINA
Equator
Tropic of Capricorn
N
0 500 1000 Miles
0 500 1000 1500 Kilometers
140°W
120°W
100°W
80°W
60°W
40°W
20°W
0°
20°N
20°S
40°S

LATIN AMERICA: Population Density
People per square mile
People per square kilometer
0–2 | 0–1
2–25 | 1–10
25–125 | 10–50
125–250 | 50–100
250–500 | 100–200
over 500 | over 200
• Cities with more than 1 million people
0 500 1000 Miles
0 500 1000 1500 Kilometers
UNITED STATES
MEXICO
Monterrey
Guadalajara
Mexico City
Gulf of Mexico
Havana
CUBA
JAMAICA
HAITI
DOMINICAN REPUBLIC
PUERTO RICO (U.S.)
BELIZE
GUATEMALA
HONDURAS
EL SALVADOR
NICARAGUA
Managua
COSTA RICA
PANAMA
Caribbean Sea
Maracaibo
Valencia
Caracas
VENEZUELA
GUYANA
SURINAME
FRENCH GUIANA
Medellín
Bogotá
Cali
COLOMBIA
ECUADOR
Quito
Guayaquil
PERU
Lima
BRAZIL
Fortaleza
Recife
Salvador
Brasília
Belo Horizonte
Rio de Janeiro
São Paulo
Curitiba
Pôrto Alegre
La Paz
BOLIVIA
PARAGUAY
CHILE
Santiago
ARGENTINA
Buenos Aires
URUGUAY
Montevideo
PACIFIC OCEAN
ATLANTIC OCEAN
Tropic of Cancer
Equator
Tropic of Capricorn
140°W
120°W
60°W
40°W
20°W
20°N
0°
20°S
40°S
N

LATIN AMERICA

Country	Capital	Area in sq mi (sq km)	Population
Antigua/Barbuda	St. John's	170 (440)	100,000
Argentina	Buenos Aires	1,068,299 (2,766,890)	32,700,000
Bahamas	Nassau	5,382 (13,940)	300,000
Barbados	Bridgetown	166 (430)	300,000
Belize	Belmopan	8,865 (22,960)	200,000
Bolivia	La Paz; Sucre	424,163 (1,098,580)	7,500,000
Brazil	Brasilia	3,286,480 (8,511,970)	153,300,000
Chile	Santiago	292,259 (756,950)	13,400,000
Colombia	Bogotá	439,734 (1,138,910)	33,600,000
Costa Rica	San José	19,652 (50,900)	3,100,000
Cuba	Havana	42,803 (110,860)	10,700,000
Dominica	Roseau	290 (750)	100,000
Dominican Republic	Santo Domingo	18,816 (48,730)	7,300,000
Ecuador	Quito	109,483 (283,560)	10,800,000
El Salvador	San Salvador	8,124 (21,040)	5,400,000
French Guiana	Cayenne	35,135 (91,000)	100,000
Grenada	St. George's	131 (340)	100,000
Guatemala	Guatemala City	42,042 (108,890)	9,500,000
Guyana	Georgetown	83,000 (214,970)	800,000
Haiti	Port-au-Prince	10,714 (27,750)	6,300,000
Honduras	Tegucigalpa	43,277 (112,090)	5,300,000
Jamaica	Kingston	4,243 (10,990)	2,500,000
Mexico	Mexico City	761,604 (1,972,550)	85,700,000
Nicaragua	Managua	49,998 (129,494)	3,900,000
Panama	Panama City	30,193 (78,200)	2,500,000
Paraguay	Asunción	157,047 (406,750)	4,400,000
Peru	Lima	496,225 (1,285,200)	22,000,000
Puerto Rico	San Juan	3,515 (9,104)	3,500,000
St. Kitts and Nevis	Basseterre	139 (360)	40,000
St. Lucia	Castries	239 (620)	200,000
St. Vincent/Grenadines	Kingstown	131 (340)	100,000
Suriname	Paramaribo	63,039 (163,270)	400,000
Trinidad/Tobago	Port-of-Spain	1,980 (5,130)	1,300,000
Uruguay	Montevideo	68,039 (175,220)	3,100,000
Venezuela	Caracas	352,143 (912,050)	20,100,000

EUROPE AND NORTHERN ASIA

Europe and Northern Asia make up the second-largest region in the world. Most of this region was once occupied by the Soviet Union. In 1991 the Soviet Union broke up into 15 independent nations. However, one of these nations—Russia—is still the largest country in the world, spanning two continents and eleven different time zones. While people in western Russia are eating dinner, people in eastern Russia are waking up the next morning!

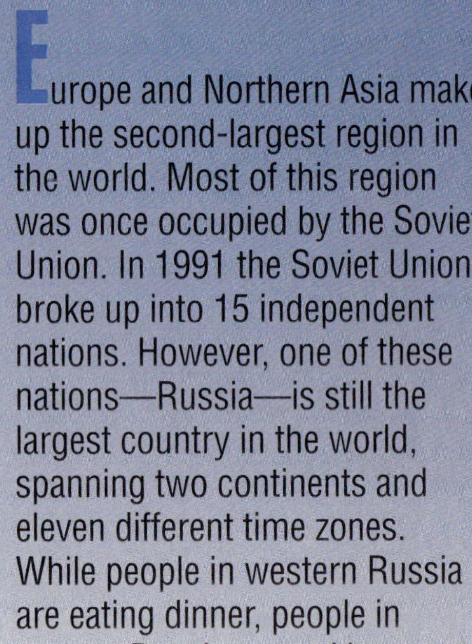

Europe forms only a very small part of this region. More than

The region of Europe and Northern Asia is home to many different peoples.

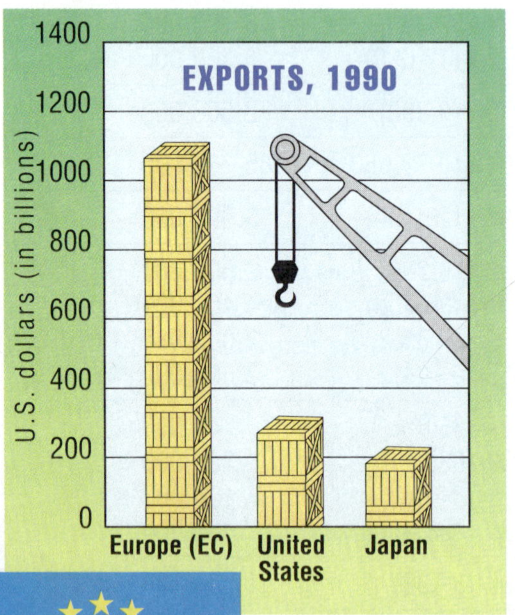

Twelve European countries form a special trade partnership called the European Community (EC). As the graph shows, the EC plays a major role in world trade.

The Eiffel Tower in Paris, France (*left*) is one of the most famous landmarks of this region.

forty countries make up an area that is about one half the size of the United States. Despite their sizes, however, these countries have played enormous roles throughout world history.

The location of Europe and Northern Asia has helped this region to play an important part in world affairs. As you look at the maps on the following pages, take special note of how the continents of Europe and Asia come together in this region. Then make some conclusions about how this link between two continents may have helped the region to grow in power and influence throughout history.

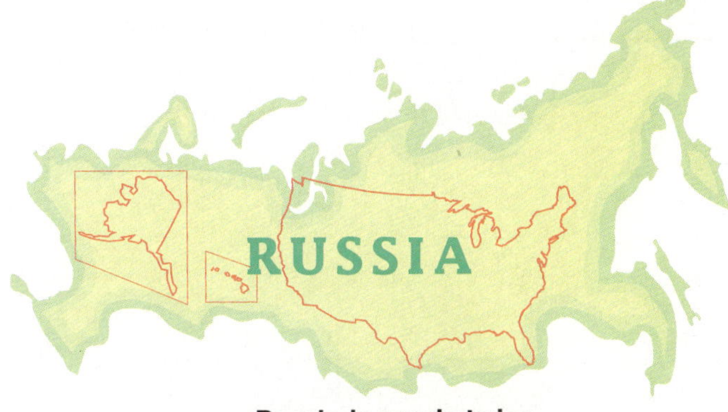

Russia is nearly twice the size of the entire United States in land area.

A 32-mile (51-km) railroad tunnel is being built under the English Channel. When the "chunnel" is completed, it will provide the first train link between England and the rest of Europe.

St. Basil's Cathedral *(right)* is located in the heart of Moscow, the capital of Russia.

Every year thousands of people come to see St. Peter's Square in Vatican City (*left*).

The Caucasus Mountains form part of the southern border of Russia.

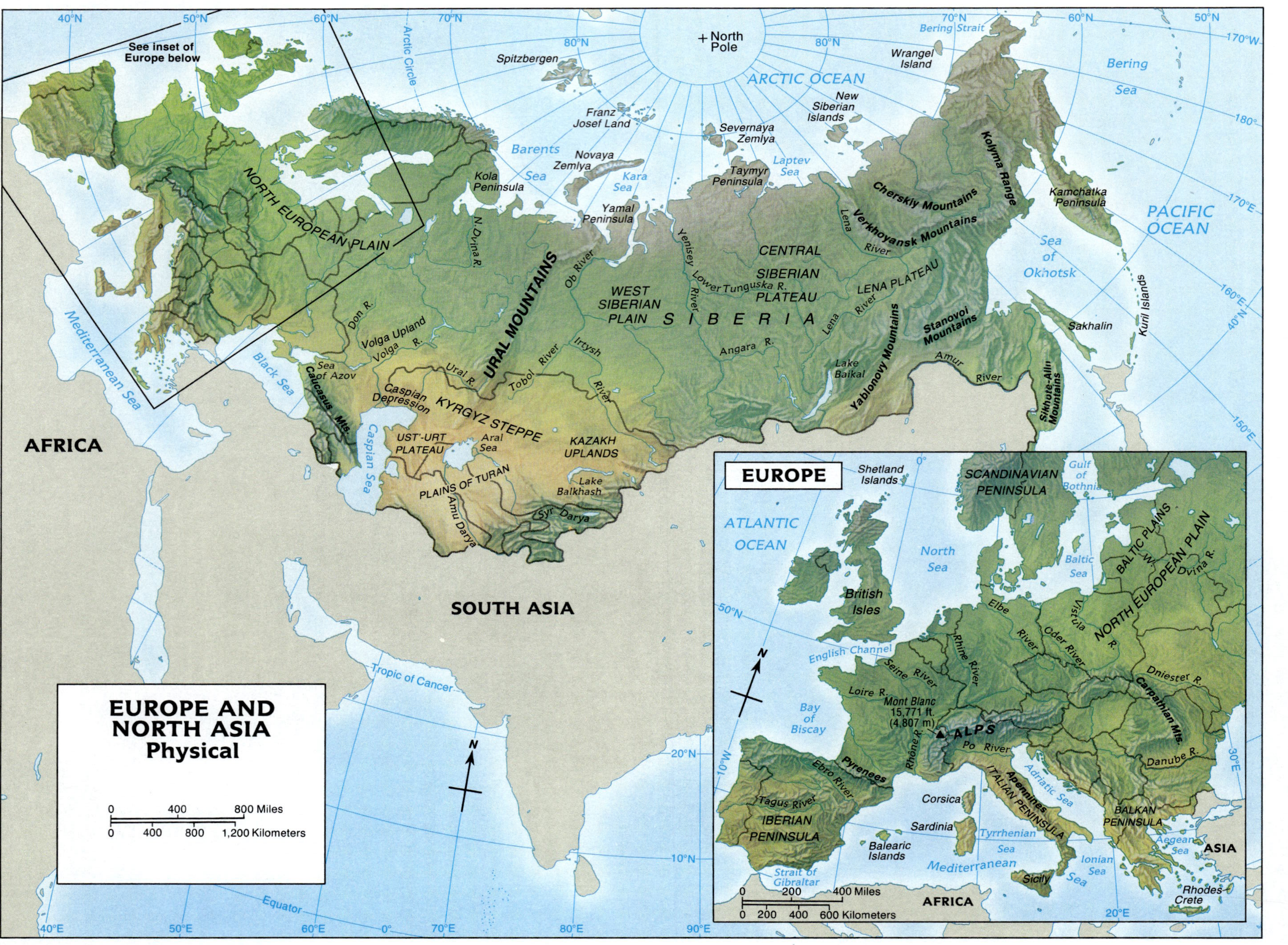
EUROPE AND NORTH ASIA
Physical
0 400 800 Miles
0 400 800 1,200 Kilometers
See inset of Europe below
NORTH EUROPEAN PLAIN
Arctic Circle
Spitzbergen
Franz Josef Land
Novaya Zemlya
Barents Sea
Kara Sea
Kola Peninsula
Yamal Peninsula
N. Dvina R.
+ North Pole
ARCTIC OCEAN
Severnaya Zemlya
Taymyr Peninsula
Laptev Sea
New Siberian Islands
Wrangel Island
Bering Strait
Bering Sea
PACIFIC OCEAN
Kamchatka Peninsula
Kolyma Range
Cherskiy Mountains
Verkhoyansk Mountains
Lena River
Sea of Okhotsk
Kuril Islands
Sakhalin
Sikhote-Alin Mountains
Stanovoi Mountains
Amur River
LENA PLATEAU
CENTRAL SIBERIAN PLATEAU
Lower Tunguska R.
Yenisey River
Lena River
Lake Baikal
Yablonovy Mountains
Angara R.
S I B E R I A
WEST SIBERIAN PLAIN
Ob River
Irtysh River
Tobol River
URAL MOUNTAINS
Ural R.
Volga Upland
Volga R.
Don R.
Sea of Azov
Caucasus Mts.
Black Sea
Caspian Depression
KYRGYZ STEPPE
Caspian Sea
UST'-URT PLATEAU
Aral Sea
PLAINS OF TURAN
Amu Darya
Syr Darya
KAZAKH UPLANDS
Lake Balkhash
Mediterranean Sea
AFRICA
SOUTH ASIA
Tropic of Cancer
Equator
EUROPE
ATLANTIC OCEAN
Shetland Islands
SCANDINAVIAN PENINSULA
Gulf of Bothnia
North Sea
Baltic Sea
BALTIC PLAINS
W. Dvina R.
NORTH EUROPEAN PLAIN
British Isles
English Channel
Elbe River
Vistula R.
Oder River
Rhine River
Seine River
Loire R.
Mont Blanc 15,771 ft. (4,807 m)
ALPS
Po River
Rhone R.
Bay of Biscay
Pyrenees
Ebro River
Tagus River
IBERIAN PENINSULA
Strait of Gibraltar
Balearic Islands
Corsica
Sardinia
Tyrrhenian Sea
Apennines
ITALIAN PENINSULA
Adriatic Sea
Sicily
Mediterranean Sea
Ionian Sea
Dniester R.
Carpathian Mts.
Danube R.
BALKAN PENINSULA
Aegean Sea
ASIA
Rhodes
Crete
AFRICA
0 200 400 Miles
0 200 400 600 Kilometers

EUROPE AND NORTH ASIA
Political
National capital
Other city
0 400 800 Miles
0 400 800 1,200 Kilometers
See inset of Europe below
North Pole
ARCTIC OCEAN
PACIFIC OCEAN
Bering Sea
Sea of Okhotsk
Barents Sea
SVALBARD (NORWAY)
FRANZ JOSEF LAND (RUSSIA)
Novaya Zemlya
Severnaya Zemlya
Kuril Islands
Sakhalin
NORWAY
SWEDEN
FINLAND
Murmansk
Archangel'sk
Arctic Circle
N. Dvina R.
Moscow
Nizhniy Novgorod (Gorki)
Kazan
Kharkov
Saratov
Samara
Yekaterinburg
Orenburg
Magnitogorsk
Orsk
Omsk
Novosibirsk
Krasnoyarsk
Irkutsk
Ulan Ude
Chila
Yakutsk
Khabarovsk
Vladivostok
Semipalatinsk
Karaganda
Alma-Ata
Bishkek
Tashkent
Dushanbe
Ashkhabad
Baku
Tbilisi
Yerevan
Rostov
Volgograd
UKRAINE
GEORGIA
ARMENIA
AZERBAIJAN
TURKMENISTAN
UZBEKISTAN
KYRGYZSTAN
TAJIKISTAN
KAZAKHSTAN
RUSSIA
SIBERIA
Ob River
Yenisey River
Lena River
Amur River
Lake Baikal
Lake Balkhash
Aral Sea
Syr Darya
Amu Darya
Ural R.
Volga R.
Don R.
Caspian Sea
Black Sea
Mediterranean Sea
AFRICA
SOUTH ASIA
Tropic of Cancer
Equator
EUROPE
ATLANTIC OCEAN
North Sea
Baltic Sea
Bay of Biscay
Mediterranean Sea
IRELAND
Dublin
Belfast
UNITED KINGDOM
Glasgow
Edinburgh
Liverpool
London
NETHERLANDS
Amsterdam
BELGIUM
Brussels
LUXEMBOURG
FRANCE
Le Havre
Paris
Nantes
Lyon
Marseille
MONACO
ANDORRA
SWITZERLAND
Bern
Zürich
LIECHTENSTEIN
GERMANY
Hamburg
Berlin
Bonn
DENMARK
Copenhagen
NORWAY
Oslo
SWEDEN
Stockholm
FINLAND
Helsinki
ESTONIA
Tallinn
LATVIA
Riga
LITHUANIA
Vilnius
(RUSSIA)
POLAND
Warsaw
Lodz
BYELARUS
Minsk
RUSSIA
St. Petersburg (Leningrad)
UKRAINE
Kiev
Odessa
MOLDOVA
Kishinev
CZECHOSLOVAKIA
CZECH REP.
SLOVAK REP.
Prague
Bratislava
AUSTRIA
Vienna
HUNGARY
Budapest
SLOVENIA
Ljubljana
CROATIA
Zagreb
BOSNIA AND HERZEGOVINA
Sarajevo
SERBIA
MONTENEGRO
YUGOSLAVIA
Belgrade
ROMANIA
Bucharest
BULGARIA
Sofia
MACEDONIA
Skopje
ALBANIA
Tiranë
GREECE
Athens
CRETE (GR.)
ASIA
ITALY
Milan
Florence
SAN MARINO
Rome
Naples
SICILY (IT.)
MALTA
SARDINIA (IT.)
CORSICA (FR.)
SPAIN
Madrid
Barcelona
Valencia
Seville
GIBRALTAR (U.K.)
BALEARIC ISLANDS (SP.)
PORTUGAL
Porto
Lisbon
Ebro River
Seine R.
Loire R.
Rhône R.
Rhine R.
Elbe R.
Danube R.
Po R.
Dnieper R.
Dniester R.
AFRICA
0 200 400 Miles
0 200 400 600 Kilometers

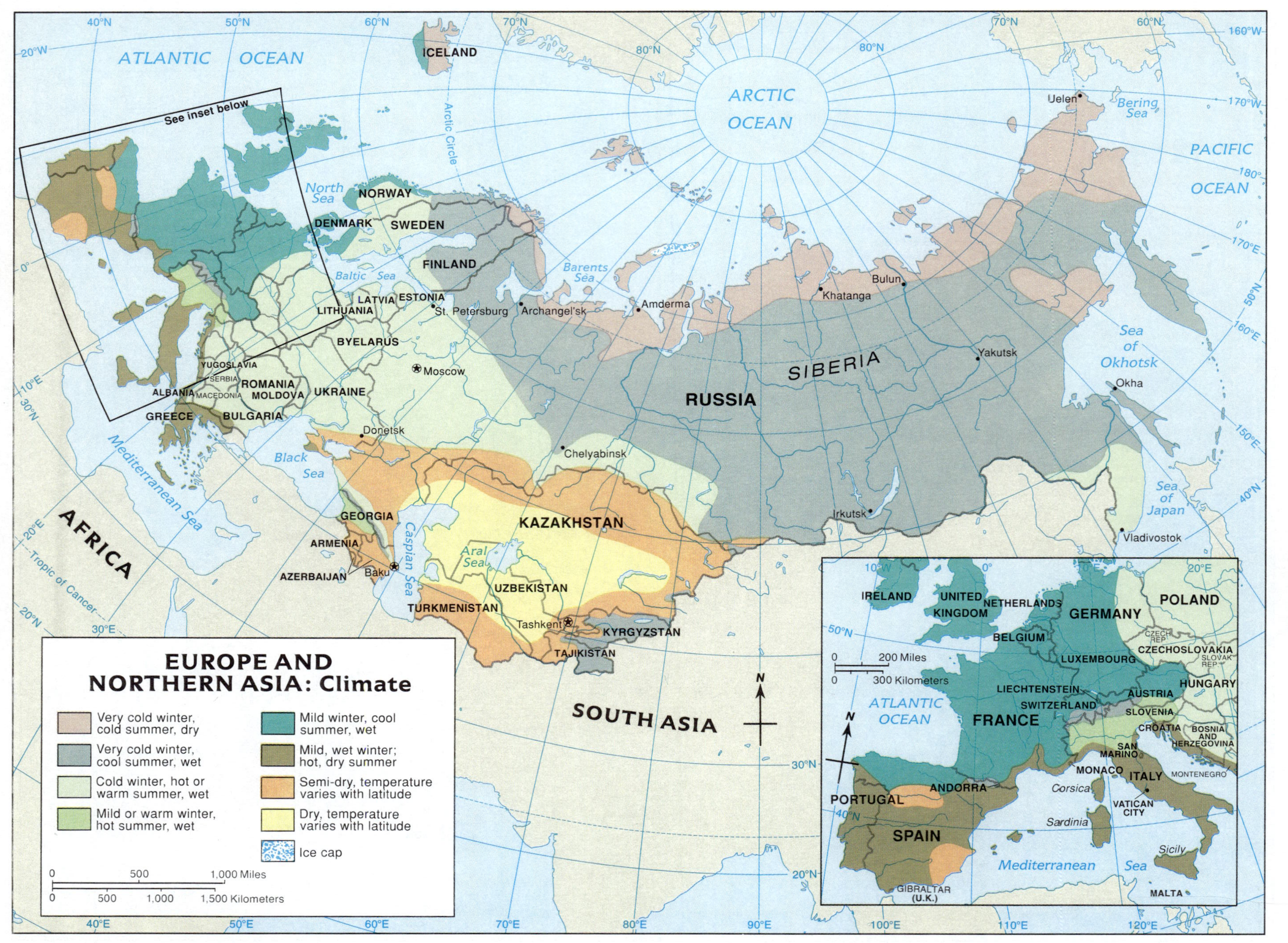
EUROPE AND NORTHERN ASIA: Climate
Very cold winter, cold summer, dry
Very cold winter, cool summer, wet
Cold winter, hot or warm summer, wet
Mild or warm winter, hot summer, wet
Mild winter, cool summer, wet
Mild, wet winter; hot, dry summer
Semi-dry, temperature varies with latitude
Dry, temperature varies with latitude
Ice cap
0 500 1,000 Miles
0 500 1,000 1,500 Kilometers
ATLANTIC OCEAN
ARCTIC OCEAN
PACIFIC OCEAN
Bering Sea
ICELAND
See inset below
Arctic Circle
North Sea
NORWAY
SWEDEN
DENMARK
FINLAND
Baltic Sea
LATVIA
ESTONIA
LITHUANIA
St. Petersburg
Archangel'sk
Barents Sea
Amderma
Khatanga
Bulun
Uelen
BYELARUS
Moscow
YUGOSLAVIA
SERBIA
ROMANIA
MOLDOVA
UKRAINE
ALBANIA
MACEDONIA
GREECE
BULGARIA
Donetsk
Black Sea
Mediterranean Sea
AFRICA
Tropic of Cancer
GEORGIA
ARMENIA
AZERBAIJAN
Baku
Caspian Sea
Aral Sea
KAZAKHSTAN
UZBEKISTAN
TURKMENISTAN
Tashkent
KYRGYZSTAN
TAJIKISTAN
Chelyabinsk
RUSSIA
SIBERIA
Yakutsk
Sea of Okhotsk
Okha
Sea of Japan
Vladivostok
Irkutsk
SOUTH ASIA
N
IRELAND
UNITED KINGDOM
NETHERLANDS
BELGIUM
GERMANY
POLAND
CZECH REP.
CZECHOSLOVAKIA
SLOVAK REP.
LUXEMBOURG
LIECHTENSTEIN
SWITZERLAND
AUSTRIA
HUNGARY
SLOVENIA
CROATIA
BOSNIA AND HERZEGOVINA
SAN MARINO
MONACO
ITALY
MONTENEGRO
VATICAN CITY
Corsica
Sardinia
Sicily
MALTA
FRANCE
ANDORRA
PORTUGAL
SPAIN
GIBRALTAR (U.K.)
ATLANTIC OCEAN
Mediterranean Sea
0 200 Miles
0 300 Kilometers

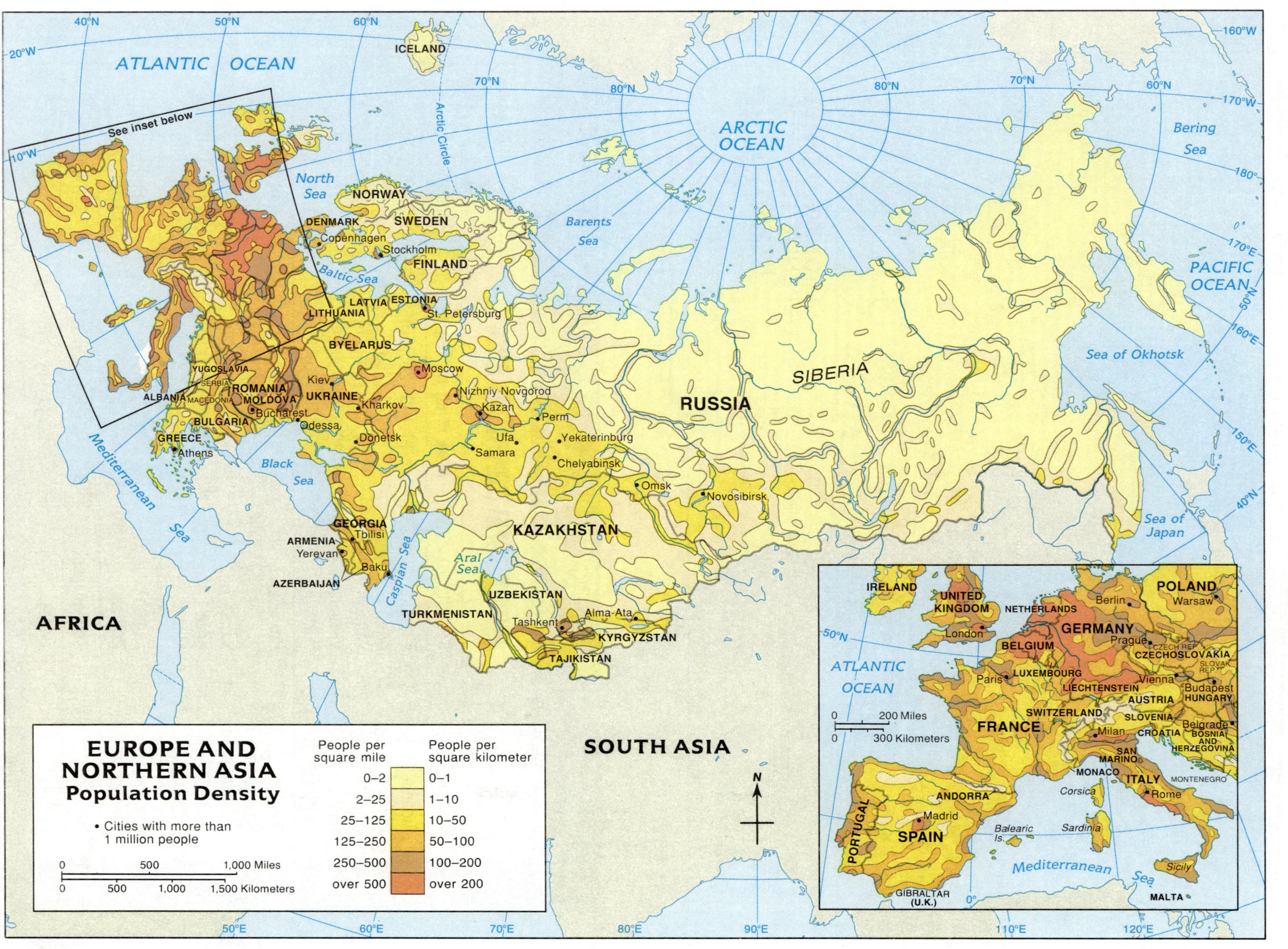
EUROPE AND NORTHERN ASIA
Population Density
• Cities with more than 1 million people
0 500 1,000 Miles
0 500 1,000 1,500 Kilometers
People per square mile
People per square kilometer
0–2 0–1
2–25 1–10
25–125 10–50
125–250 50–100
250–500 100–200
over 500 over 200
ATLANTIC OCEAN
ICELAND
Arctic Circle
ARCTIC OCEAN
Bering Sea
PACIFIC OCEAN
Sea of Okhotsk
Sea of Japan
Barents Sea
North Sea
Baltic Sea
Black Sea
Caspian Sea
Aral Sea
Mediterranean Sea
See inset below
NORWAY
SWEDEN
DENMARK
Copenhagen
Stockholm
FINLAND
ESTONIA
LATVIA
LITHUANIA
St. Petersburg
BYELARUS
Moscow
Kiev
UKRAINE
Kharkov
Nizhniy Novgorod
Kazan
Perm
Ufa
Samara
Yekaterinburg
Chelyabinsk
Omsk
Novosibirsk
Donetsk
Odessa
YUGOSLAVIA
SERBIA
ROMANIA
MOLDOVA
Bucharest
ALBANIA
MACEDONIA
BULGARIA
GREECE
Athens
SIBERIA
RUSSIA
KAZAKHSTAN
GEORGIA
Tbilisi
ARMENIA
Yerevan
Baku
AZERBAIJAN
UZBEKISTAN
TURKMENISTAN
Tashkent
Alma-Ata
KYRGYZSTAN
TAJIKISTAN
AFRICA
SOUTH ASIA
N
IRELAND
UNITED KINGDOM
London
NETHERLANDS
BELGIUM
LUXEMBOURG
Paris
GERMANY
Berlin
POLAND
Warsaw
Prague
CZECH REP.
CZECHOSLOVAKIA
SLOVAK REP.
LIECHTENSTEIN
Vienna
AUSTRIA
Budapest
HUNGARY
SWITZERLAND
SLOVENIA
CROATIA
Belgrade
BOSNIA AND HERZEGOVINA
FRANCE
Milan
SAN MARINO
MONACO
ITALY
MONTENEGRO
Rome
Corsica
Sardinia
Sicily
MALTA
ANDORRA
PORTUGAL
Madrid
SPAIN
Balearic Is.
GIBRALTAR (U.K.)
ATLANTIC OCEAN
Mediterranean Sea
0 200 Miles
0 300 Kilometers
40°N
50°N
60°N
70°N
80°N
20°W
10°W
0°
50°E
60°E
70°E
80°E
90°E
110°E
120°E
150°E
160°E
170°E
180°
170°W
160°W

EUROPE AND NORTHERN ASIA

Country	Capital	Area in sq mi (sq km)	Population
Albania	Tiranë	11,100 (28,750)	3,300,000
Andorra	Andorra la Vella	174 (450)	53,000
Armenia	Yerevan	11,490 (29,800)	3,300,000
Austria	Vienna	32,375 (83,850)	7,700,000
Azerbaijan	Baku	33,430 (86,600)	7,100,000
Belgium	Brussels	11,779 (30,510)	9,900,000
Bosnia and Herzegovina	Sarajevo	19,741 (51,129)	4,100,000
Bulgaria	Sofia	42,822 (110,910)	9,000,000
Byelarus	Minsk	80,134 (207,600)	10,300,000
Croatia	Zagreb	21,829 (56,537)	4,600,000
Czechoslovakia	Prague	49,365 (127,870)	15,700,000
Denmark	Copenhagen	16,629 (43,070)	5,100,000
Estonia	Tallinn	17,413 (45,100)	1,600,000

Finland	Helsinki	130,128 (337,030)	5,000,000
France	Paris	211,209 (547,030)	56,700,000
Georgia	Tbilisi	26,900 (69,700)	5,500,000
Germany	Berlin	137,803 (356,910)	79,500,000
Greece	Athens	50,942 (131,940)	10,100,000
Hungary	Budapest	35,919 (93,030)	10,400,000
Iceland	Reykjavik	39,768 (103,000)	300,000
Ireland	Dublin	27,135 (70,820)	3,500,000
Italy	Rome	116,305 (301,230)	57,700,000
Kazakhstan	Alma-Ata	1,049,155 (2,717,300)	16,700,000
Kyrgyzstan	Bishkek	76,640 (198,500)	4,400,000
Latvia	Riga	24,595 (63,700)	2,700,000
Liechtenstein	Vaduz	62 (160)	30,000
Lithuania	Vilnius	25,170 (65,200)	3,700,000
Luxembourg	Luxembourg	998 (2,586)	400,000
Macedonia	Skopje	9,928 (25,713)	1,900,000
Malta	Valletta	123 (320)	400,000
Moldova	Kishinev	13,000 (33,700)	4,400,000
Monaco	Monaco	0.7 (1.9)	30,000
Netherlands, The	Amsterdam	14,405 (37,310)	15,000,000
Norway	Oslo	125,182 (324,220)	4,300,000
Poland	Warsaw	120,726 (312,680)	38,200,000
Portugal	Lisbon	35,552 (92,080)	10,400,000
Romania	Bucharest	91,699 (237,500)	23,400,000
Russia	Moscow	6,592,813 (17,075,000)	148,000,000
San Marino	San Marino	23 (60)	23,000
Slovenia	Ljubljana	7,819 (20,251)	1,900,000
Spain	Madrid	194,884 (504,750)	39,000,000
Sweden	Stockholm	173,730 (449,960)	8,600,000
Switzerland	Bern	15,942 (41,290)	6,800,000
Tajikistan	Dushanbe	55,240 (143,100)	5,300,000
Turkmenistan	Ashkhabad	186,400 (488,100)	3,600,000
Ukraine	Kiev	231,990 (445,000)	51,800,000
United Kingdom	London	94,525 (244,820)	57,500,000
Uzbekistan	Tashkent	172,741 (447,400)	20,300,000
Vatican City	Vatican City	0.17 (0.44)	750
Yugoslavia	Belgrade	39,449 (102,173)	10,200,000

MIDDLE EAST AND NORTH AFRICA

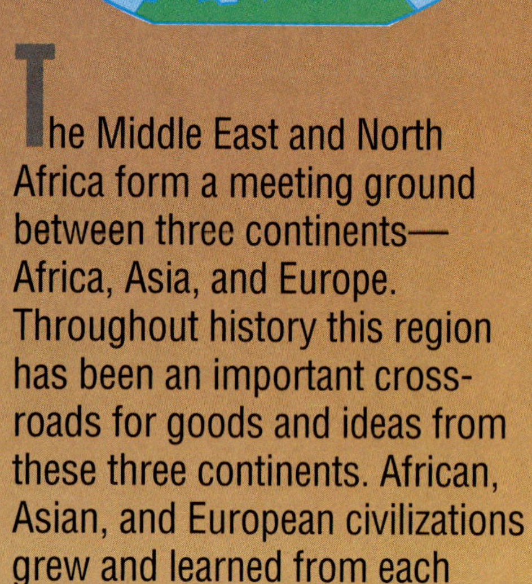

The Middle East and North Africa form a meeting ground between three continents—Africa, Asia, and Europe. Throughout history this region has been an important crossroads for goods and ideas from these three continents. African, Asian, and European civilizations grew and learned from each other because of the traders who crossed the seas, deserts, and mountains of this region.

Along with fertile river valleys and plains, this region includes some of the hottest, driest places on earth. It gets so hot, in fact,

This Israeli farm boy, Arab student, and North African shepherd girl represent three of the groups that live in the Middle East and North Africa.

Israel is a leading exporter of citrus fruits. There, crops are grown on land reclaimed from the desert.

Saudi Arabia is about one third the size of the 48 states of the continental United States.

that thermometers have burst in the midday sun! Not surprisingly, water is a precious natural resource throughout the region.

Another important natural resource is oil. Oil has brought great wealth to parts of this region. But it has also caused much conflict as people struggle for control over this valuable resource.

As you look at the maps of this region, identify the countries that have benefited the most from oil production in the Middle East and North Africa. Also try to determine how the need for water has shaped settlement in this region.

WORLD'S HOTTEST PLACE

Degrees Fahrenheit	Degrees Celsius
136	57
104	40
50	10
32	0

The hottest place on earth is Al'Aziziyah, Libya. In 1922 a temperature of 136°F. (57°C) was recorded there.

Today, Egypt's pyramids remind us of the ancient civilization that once ruled the Nile River Valley.

Jerusalem is an important city for people of three different religious faiths.

Egypt's Suez Canal, 105 miles (168 km) long, is one of the world's most important human-made waterways. It first opened in 1869.

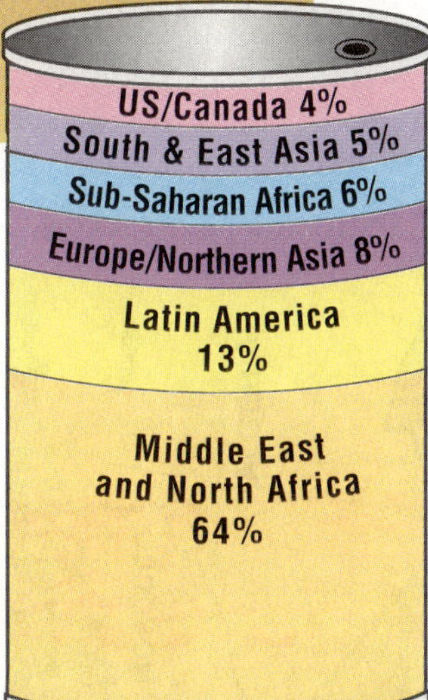

WORLD OIL RESERVES

Oil has made the Middle East and North Africa one of the wealthiest regions in the world. Use the chart to learn the percentage of the world's oil reserves found in this region.

The Aswan Dam, on the Nile River in Egypt, provides a steady water supply for many farmers.

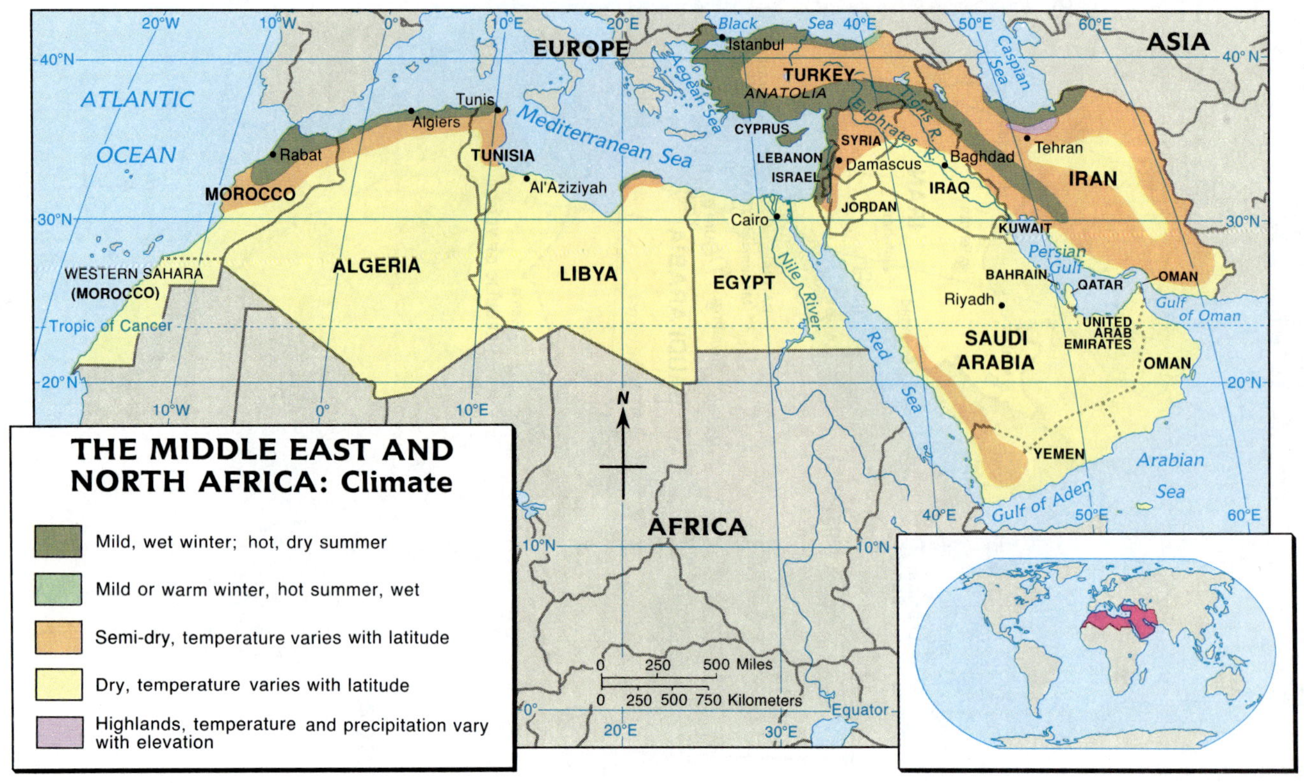
THE MIDDLE EAST AND NORTH AFRICA: Climate
Mild, wet winter; hot, dry summer
Mild or warm winter, hot summer, wet
Semi-dry, temperature varies with latitude
Dry, temperature varies with latitude
Highlands, temperature and precipitation vary with elevation
ATLANTIC OCEAN
EUROPE
ASIA
AFRICA
Mediterranean Sea
Black Sea
Caspian Sea
Aegean Sea
Red Sea
Persian Gulf
Gulf of Oman
Arabian Sea
Gulf of Aden
Nile River
Euphrates R.
Tigris R.
MOROCCO
WESTERN SAHARA (MOROCCO)
ALGERIA
TUNISIA
LIBYA
EGYPT
TURKEY
ANATOLIA
CYPRUS
LEBANON
ISRAEL
SYRIA
JORDAN
IRAQ
IRAN
KUWAIT
BAHRAIN
QATAR
SAUDI ARABIA
UNITED ARAB EMIRATES
OMAN
YEMEN
Rabat
Algiers
Tunis
Al'Aziziyah
Cairo
Istanbul
Damascus
Baghdad
Tehran
Riyadh
Tropic of Cancer
Equator
0 250 500 Miles
0 250 500 750 Kilometers
N

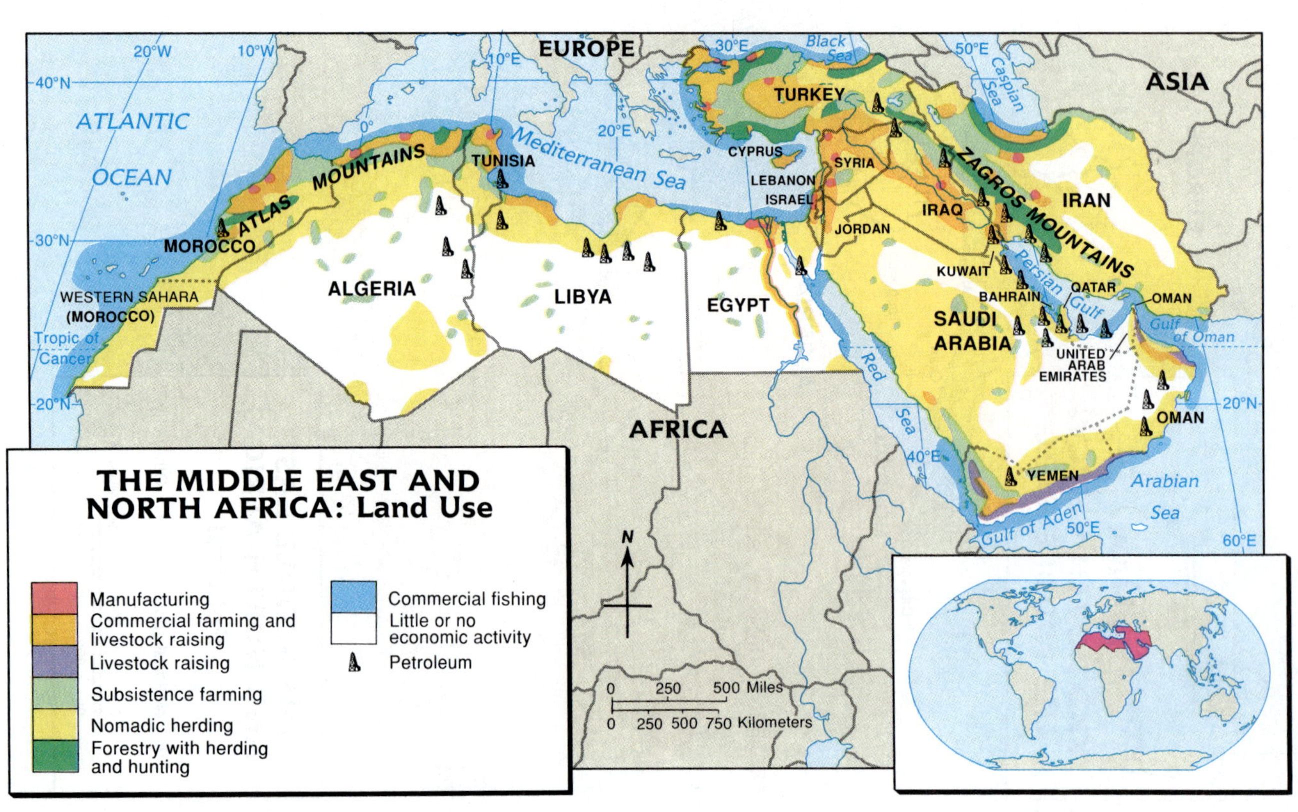
THE MIDDLE EAST AND NORTH AFRICA: Land Use
Manufacturing
Commercial farming and livestock raising
Livestock raising
Subsistence farming
Nomadic herding
Forestry with herding and hunting
Commercial fishing
Little or no economic activity
Petroleum
ATLANTIC OCEAN
EUROPE
ASIA
AFRICA
Mediterranean Sea
Black Sea
Caspian Sea
Red Sea
Persian Gulf
Gulf of Oman
Arabian Sea
Gulf of Aden
ATLAS MOUNTAINS
ZAGROS MOUNTAINS
MOROCCO
WESTERN SAHARA (MOROCCO)
ALGERIA
TUNISIA
LIBYA
EGYPT
TURKEY
CYPRUS
LEBANON
ISRAEL
SYRIA
JORDAN
IRAQ
IRAN
KUWAIT
BAHRAIN
QATAR
SAUDI ARABIA
UNITED ARAB EMIRATES
OMAN
YEMEN
Tropic of Cancer
0 250 500 Miles
0 250 500 750 Kilometers
N

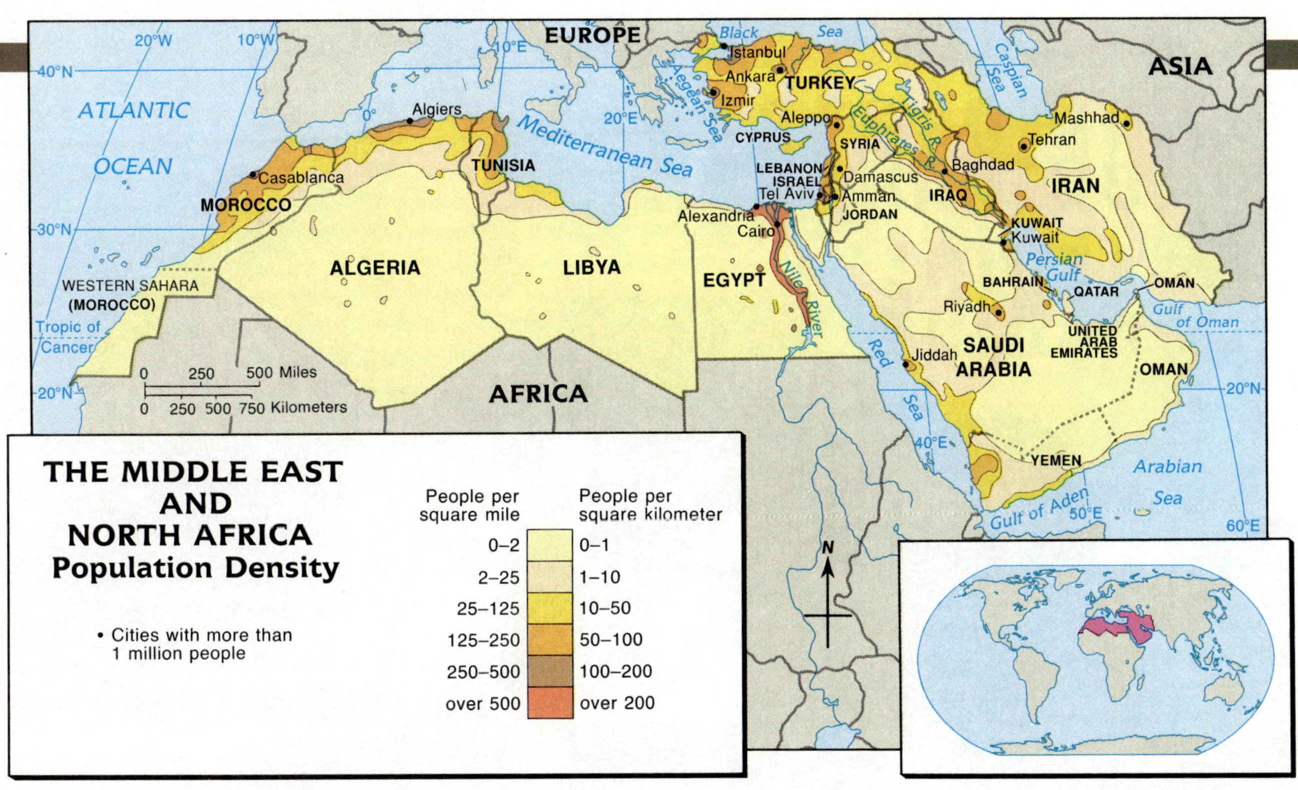

THE MIDDLE EAST AND NORTH AFRICA

Country	Capital	Area in sq mi (sq km)	Population
Algeria	Algiers	919,592 (2,381,740)	26,000,000
Bahrain	Manama	239 (620)	500,000
Cyprus	Nicosia	3,571 (9,250)	700,000
Egypt	Cairo	386,661 (1,001,450)	54,500,000
Iran	Tehran	636,294 (1,648,000)	58,600,000
Iraq	Baghdad	167,923 (434,920)	17,100,000
Israel	Jerusalem	8,091 (20,770)	4,900,000
Jordan	Amman	35,475 (91,880)	3,400,000
Kuwait	Kuwait	6,880 (17,820)	1,400,000
Lebanon	Beirut	4,015 (10,400)	3,400,000
Libya	Tripoli	679,360 (1,759,540)	4,400,000
Morocco	Rabat	172,413 (446,550)	26,200,000
Oman	Muscat	82,013 (212,460)	1,600,000
Qatar	Doha	4,247 (11,000)	500,000
Saudi Arabia	Riyadh	829,997 (2,149,690)	15,500,000
Syria	Damascus	71,498 (185,180)	12,800,000
Tunisia	Tunis	63,170 (163,610)	8,400,000
Turkey	Ankara	301,383 (780,580)	58,500,000
United Arab Emirates	Abu Dhabi	32,278 (83,600)	2,400,000
Yemen	San'a	203,850 (527,970)	10,100,000

SUB-SAHARAN AFRICA

The continent of Africa is split into two regions by the Sahara, the world's largest desert. North Africa is a hot and dry region that shares cultural ties with the Middle East. By contrast, Africa below the Sahara—or "Sub-Saharan" Africa—has many different landforms and ways of life.

Sub-Saharan Africa is a vast region that contains more land than all of North America. In some places you will find hot

As in all regions, children are the future of Sub-Saharan Africa. Almost half of the people of this region are under the age of 15.

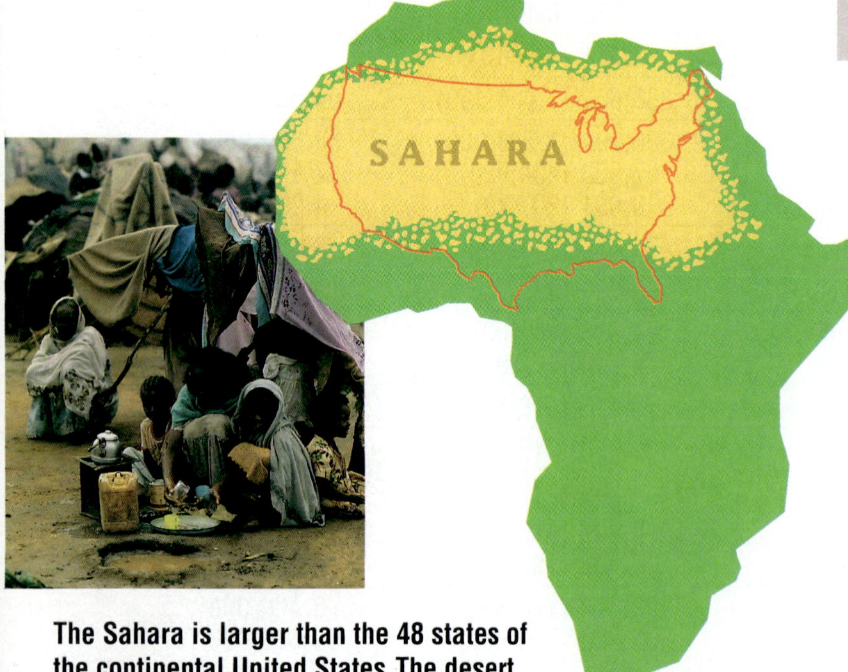

The Sahara is larger than the 48 states of the continental United States. The desert continues to grow each year, destroying farmland and causing millions of people to go hungry.

Lions, zebras, and other wildlife live on the plains below Mount Kilimanjaro, Africa's tallest mountain.

and dry landforms like those in North Africa. Elsewhere you will find rain forests, ice-capped mountains, dramatic waterfalls, and large lakes.

For some people Sub-Saharan Africa is a lush storehouse of beauty and natural resources. For many others this land they call home demands an endless struggle to survive each new day. As you look at the maps of this region, look for the many different landforms that are located in Sub-Saharan Africa.

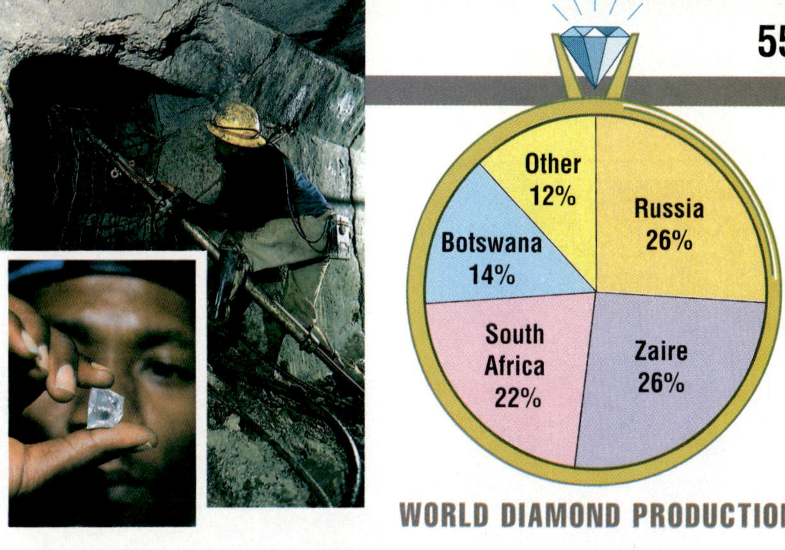

Most of the world's diamonds come from countries in Sub-Saharan Africa, as the graph shows. People work in tunnels dug deep into the earth to recover gems like the one shown above.

Sub-Saharan Africa is a region of both busy cities and small villages, such as these in West Africa.

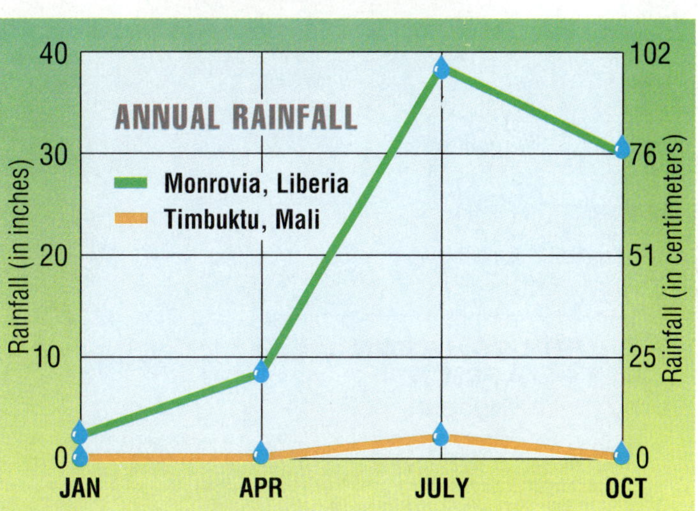

Annual rainfall varies greatly in Sub-Saharan Africa. According to the graph, how much rain falls in Monrovia, Liberia, and Timbuktu, Mali, in July?

EUROPE
ASIA
ATLANTIC OCEAN
Mediterranean Sea
Red Sea
Gulf of Aden
Tropic of Cancer
Cape Blanco
S A H A R A
AIR
NUBIAN DESERT
Nile River
Atbara R.
Blue Nile
White Nile
SUDD
Ethiopian Highlands
Somali Peninsula
Senegal River
Gambia R.
Cape Verde
Niger River
Lake Chad
Benue River
ADAMAOUA
Lake Volta
Cape Palmas
Fernando Po
Gulf of Guinea
Principe
São Tomé
Cape Lopez
Equator
Ubangi
Zaire River
CONGO BASIN
Lake Albert
Ruwenzori Range
Lake Turkana
Lake Victoria
Mt. Kilimanjaro
19,340 ft.
(5,895 m)
Pemba Island
Zanzibar Island
Kasai River
Kwango River
Lualaba River
Lake Tanganyika
Lake Nyasa
Cape Delgado
Comoro Islands
ATLANTIC OCEAN
BIE PLATEAU
Cubango River
Cuando River
Zambezi River
Lake Kariba
Victoria Falls
OKAVANGO BASIN
Mozambique Channel
Madagascar
Réunion
NAMIB DESERT
KALAHARI DESERT
Limpopo R.
Orange River
Vaal River
Drakensberg
INDIAN OCEAN
Tropic of Capricorn
Cape of Good Hope
Cape Agulhas
N
SUB-SAHARAN AFRICA Physical
0 250 500 750 Miles
0 250 500 750 1,000 Kilometers
30°W
20°W
10°W
0°
10°E
20°E
30°E
40°E
50°E
60°E
40°N
30°N
20°N
10°N
10°S
20°S
30°S
40°S

SUB-SAHARAN AFRICA Political
National capital
Other city
0 250 500 750 Miles
0 250 500 750 1,000 Kilometers
ATLANTIC OCEAN
EUROPE
ASIA
Mediterranean Sea
Red Sea
Nile River
Tropic of Cancer
Gulf of Aden
Equator
Tropic of Capricorn
INDIAN OCEAN
MAURITANIA
Nouakchott
MALI
Timbuktu
NIGER
Niamey
CHAD
N'Djamena
Lake Chad
SUDAN
Khartoum
Port Sudan
Asmara
DJIBOUTI
Djibouti
ETHIOPIA
Addis Ababa
SOMALIA
Mogadishu
SENEGAL
Dakar
Banjul
GAMBIA
Senegal River
Niger River
Bissau
GUINEA-BISSAU
GUINEA
Conakry
Freetown
SIERRA LEONE
Monrovia
LIBERIA
BURKINA FASO
Bamako
Ouagadougou
CÔTE D'IVOIRE (IVORY COAST)
Abidjan
GHANA
Lake Volta
Accra
TOGO
Lomé
BENIN
Porto-Novo
NIGERIA
Kano
Abuja
Lagos
Benue River
CAMEROON
Yaoundé
Malabo
EQUATORIAL GUINEA
SÃO TOMÉ AND PRÍNCIPE
São Tomé
CENTRAL AFRICAN REPUBLIC
Bangui
GABON
Libreville
CONGO
Brazzaville
Kinshasa
CABINDA (ANGOLA)
ZAIRE
Zaire River
Kisangani
Kananga
UGANDA
Kampala
KENYA
Nairobi
Mombasa
Lake Victoria
RWANDA
Kigali
BURUNDI
Bujumbura
TANZANIA
Dar es Salaam
Pemba
Zanzibar
Victoria
SEYCHELLES
Moroni
COMOROS
MAYOTTE (FR.)
ANGOLA
Luanda
ZAMBIA
Lusaka
Zambezi River
MALAWI
Lilongwe
ZIMBABWE
Harare
MOZAMBIQUE
Maputo
MADAGASCAR
Antananarivo
RÉUNION (FR.)
NAMIBIA
Windhoek
WALVIS BAY (S.A.)
BOTSWANA
Gaborone
Pretoria
Johannesburg
Mbabane
SWAZILAND
Orange River
Bloemfontein
Maseru
LESOTHO
Durban
SOUTH AFRICA
Cape Town
Port Elizabeth
N
30°W
20°W
10°W
0°
10°E
20°E
30°E
40°E
50°E
60°E
40°N
30°N
20°N
10°N
0°
10°S
20°S
30°S
40°S

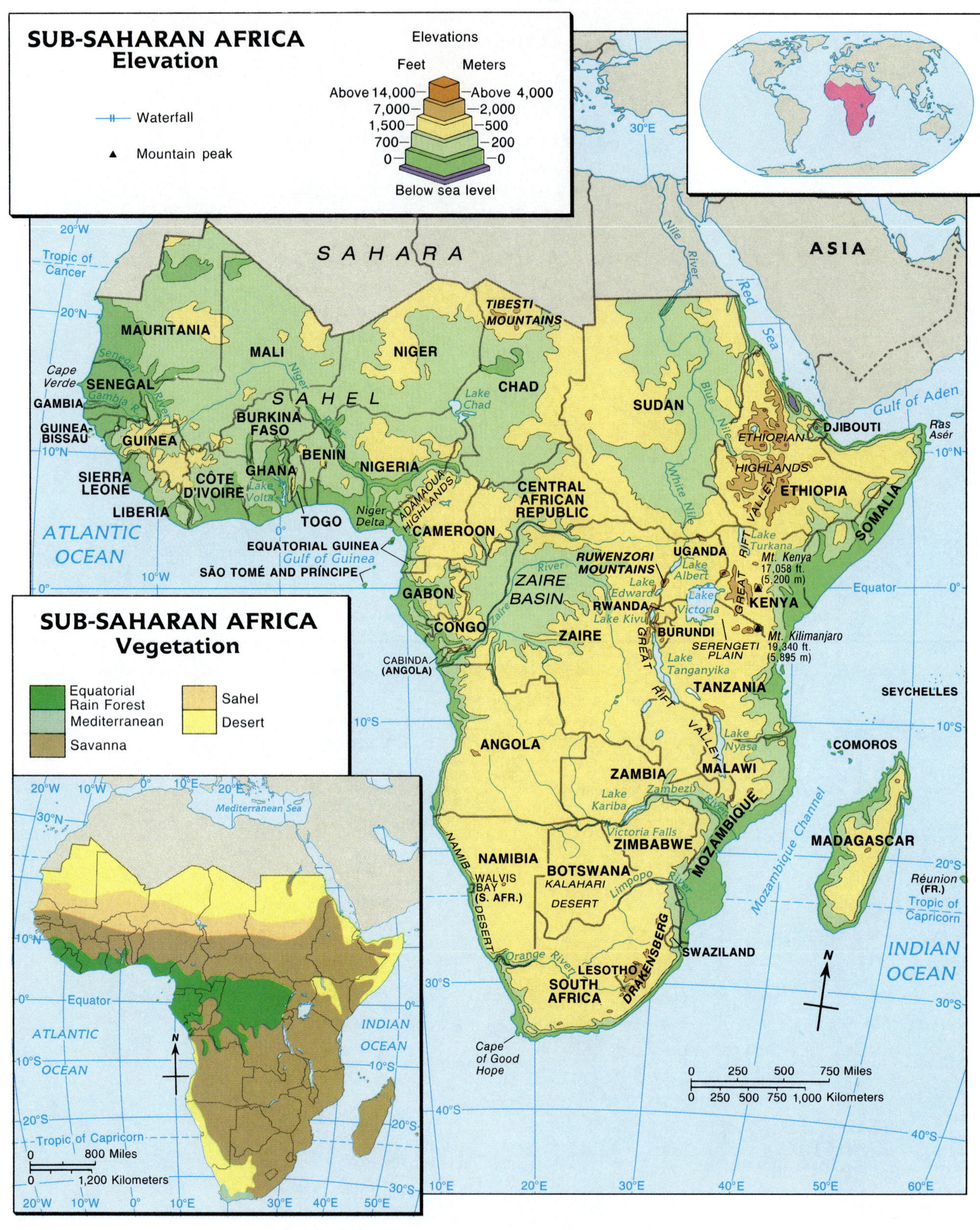
SUB-SAHARAN AFRICA
Elevation
Waterfall
Mountain peak
Elevations
Feet
Meters
Above 14,000
7,000
1,500
700
0
Above 4,000
2,000
500
200
0
Below sea level
SAHARA
ASIA
Tropic of Cancer
MAURITANIA
MALI
NIGER
TIBESTI MOUNTAINS
CHAD
SUDAN
Cape Verde
SENEGAL
GAMBIA
GUINEA-BISSAU
GUINEA
SAHEL
BURKINA FASO
BENIN
NIGERIA
SIERRA LEONE
LIBERIA
CÔTE D'IVOIRE
GHANA
Lake Volta
TOGO
Niger Delta
ADAMAOUA HIGHLANDS
CAMEROON
CENTRAL AFRICAN REPUBLIC
ETHIOPIAN HIGHLANDS
ETHIOPIA
DJIBOUTI
Ras Asér
Gulf of Aden
Red Sea
Nile River
Blue Nile
White Nile
Lake Chad
Niger River
SOMALIA
ATLANTIC OCEAN
EQUATORIAL GUINEA
Gulf of Guinea
SÃO TOMÉ AND PRÍNCIPE
GABON
CONGO
ZAIRE BASIN
RUWENZORI MOUNTAINS
UGANDA
Lake Albert
Lake Edward
RWANDA
Lake Kivu
BURUNDI
Lake Victoria
KENYA
Lake Turkana
Mt. Kenya 17,058 ft. (5,200 m)
Mt. Kilimanjaro 19,340 ft. (5,895 m)
SERENGETI PLAIN
GREAT RIFT VALLEY
ZAIRE
Lake Tanganyika
TANZANIA
CABINDA (ANGOLA)
SEYCHELLES
COMOROS
ANGOLA
ZAMBIA
MALAWI
Lake Nyasa
Lake Kariba
Zambezi River
Victoria Falls
ZIMBABWE
MOZAMBIQUE
Mozambique Channel
MADAGASCAR
NAMIBIA
NAMIB DESERT
WALVIS BAY (S. AFR.)
BOTSWANA
KALAHARI DESERT
Limpopo River
Réunion (FR.)
Tropic of Capricorn
SWAZILAND
INDIAN OCEAN
Orange River
LESOTHO
SOUTH AFRICA
DRAKENSBERG
Cape of Good Hope
Equator
0 250 500 750 Miles
0 250 500 750 1,000 Kilometers
SUB-SAHARAN AFRICA
Vegetation
Equatorial Rain Forest
Mediterranean
Savanna
Sahel
Desert
Mediterranean Sea
ATLANTIC OCEAN
INDIAN OCEAN
0 800 Miles
0 1,200 Kilometers

DESERT SURFACES OF THE SAHARA
Erg: Vast stretches of shifting sand dunes
Hammada: Worn-down rock platforms surrounding oasis
Wadi: Dry river valleys with flat bottoms
Reg: Plains covered with deposits of sand and gravel

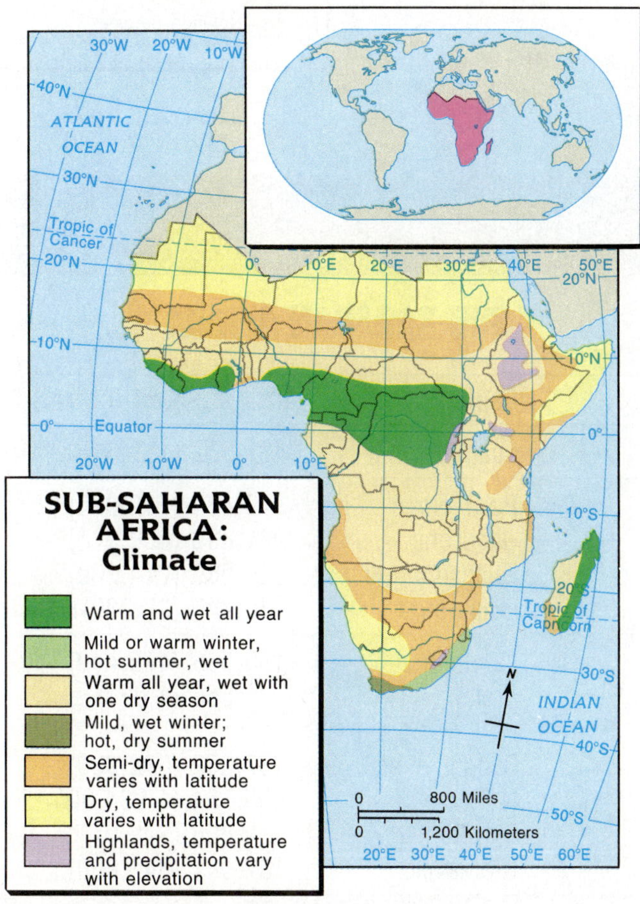
SUB-SAHARAN AFRICA: Climate
Warm and wet all year
Mild or warm winter, hot summer, wet
Warm all year, wet with one dry season
Mild, wet winter; hot, dry summer
Semi-dry, temperature varies with latitude
Dry, temperature varies with latitude
Highlands, temperature and precipitation vary with elevation
ATLANTIC OCEAN
INDIAN OCEAN
Tropic of Cancer
Tropic of Capricorn
Equator
0 800 Miles
0 1,200 Kilometers
N

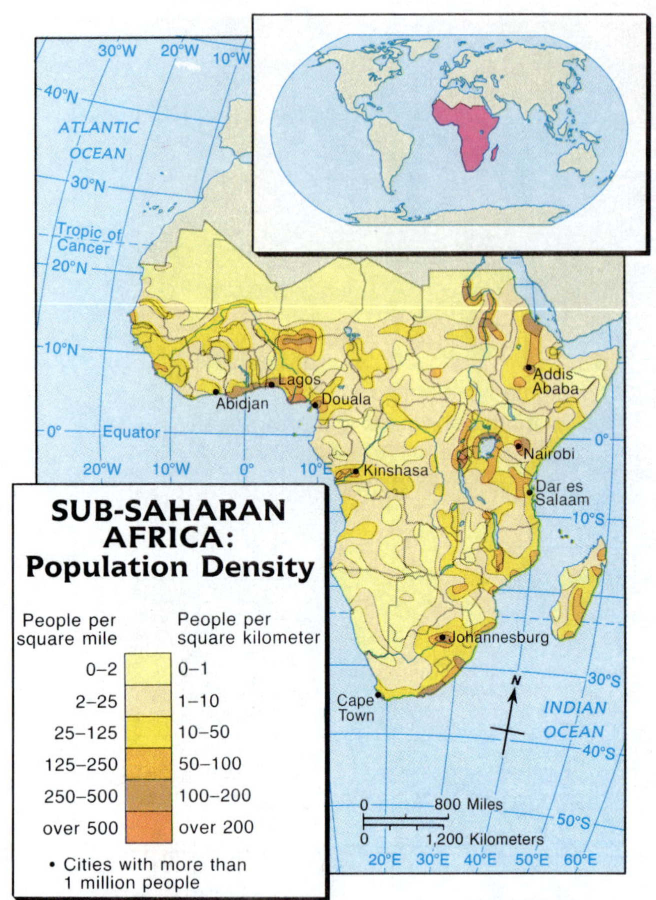

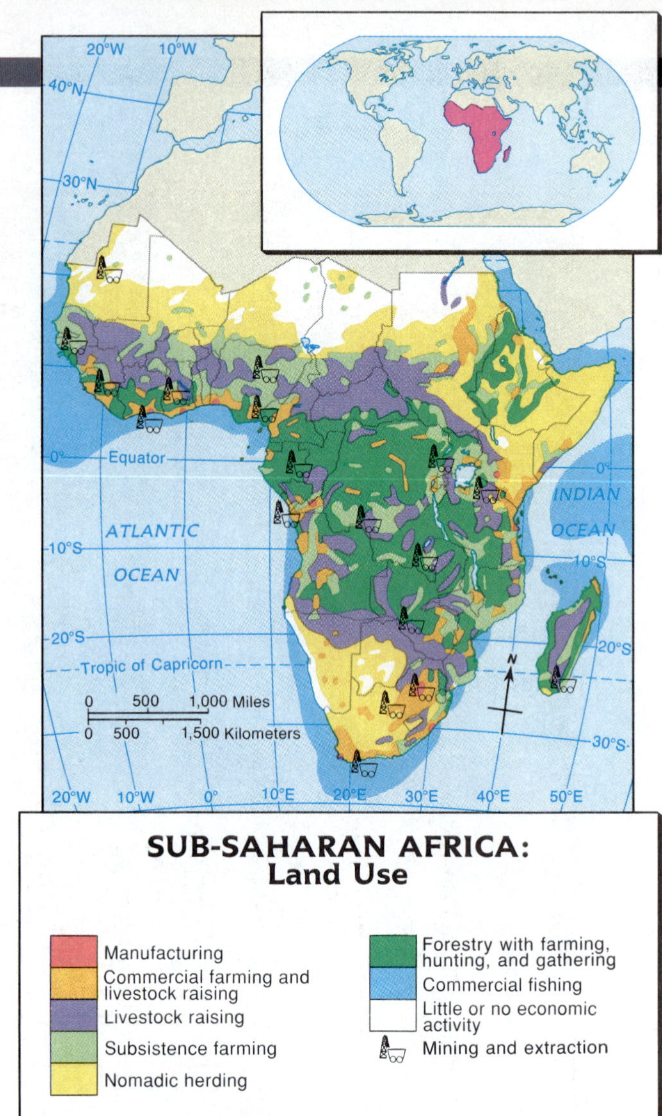

SUB-SAHARAN AFRICA

Country	Capital	Area in sq mi (sq km)	Population
Angola	Luanda	481,352 (1,246,700)	8,500,000
Benin	Porto-Novo	43,483 (112,620)	4,800,000
Botswana	Gaborone	231,803 (600,370)	1,300,000
Burkina Faso	Ouagadougou	105,869 (274,200)	9,400,000
Burundi	Bujumbura	10,745 (27,830)	5,800,000
Cameroon	Yaoundé	183,568 (475,440)	11,400,000
Cape Verde	Praia	1,556 (4,030)	400,000
Central African Republic	Bangui	237,362 (622,980)	3,000,000
Chad	N'Djamena	495,754 (1,284,000)	5,100,000
Comoros	Moroni	838 (2,170)	500,000
Congo	Brazzaville	132,047 (342,000)	2,300,000

Country	Capital	Area in sq mi (sq km)	Population
Côte d'Ivoire	Abidjan	124,502 (322,460)	12,500,000
Djibouti	Djibouti	8,494 (22,000)	400,000
Equatorial Guinea	Malabo	10,830 (28,050)	400,000
Ethiopia	Addis Ababa	471,777 (1,221,900)	53,200,000
Gabon	Libreville	103,348 (267,670)	1,200,000
Gambia, (The)	Banjul	4,363 (11,300)	900,000
Ghana	Accra	92,101 (238,540)	15,500,000
Guinea	Conakry	94,927 (245,860)	7,500,000
Guinea-Bissau	Bissau	13,946 (36,120)	1,000,000
Kenya	Nairobi	224,962 (582,650)	25,200,000
Lesotho	Maseru	11,718 (30,350)	1,800,000
Liberia	Monrovia	43,000 (111,370)	2,700,000
Madagascar	Antananarivo	226,656 (587,040)	12,400,000
Malawi	Lilongwe	45,745 (118,480)	9,400,000
Mali	Bamako	478,765 (1,240,000)	8,300,000
Mauritania	Nouakchott	397,954 (1,030,700)	2,100,000
Mauritius	Port Louis	718 (1,860)	1,100,000
Mozambique	Maputo	309,495 (801,590)	16,100,000
Namibia	Windhoek	318,259 (824,290)	1,500,000
Niger	Niamey	489,190 (1,267,000)	8,000,000
Nigeria	Abuja	356,669 (923,770)	122,500,000
Rwanda	Kigali	10,170 (26,340)	7,500,000
São Tomé and Príncipe	São Tomé	371 (960)	100,000
Senegal	Dakar	75,749 (196,190)	7,500,000
Seychelles	Victoria	171 (443)	100,000
Sierra Leone	Freetown	27,699 (71,740)	4,300,000
Somalia	Mogadishu	246,201 (637,660)	7,700,000
South Africa	Pretoria; Cape Town; Bloemfontein	471,445 (1,221,040)	40,600,000
Sudan	Khartoum	967,496 (2,505,810)	25,900,000
Swaziland	Mbabane	6,703 (17,360)	800,000
Tanzania	Dar es Salaam	364,900 (945,090)	26,900,000
Togo	Lomé	21,927 (56,790)	3,800,000
Uganda	Kampala	91,135 (236,040)	18,700,000
Zaire	Kinshasa	905,565 (2,345,410)	37,800,000
Zambia	Lusaka	290,583 (752,610)	8,400,000
Zimbabwe	Harare	150,803 (390,580)	10,000,000

SOUTHERN AND EASTERN ASIA

The continent of Asia is divided into two sections. Northern Asia includes Russia and its neighbors. (You can see maps of this area on pages 42–46.) The rest of the continent makes up the world's largest region, known as Southern and Eastern Asia. Here you will find the world's tallest mountains, some of the world's longest rivers, thousands of islands—and millions upon millions of people.

The region of Southern and Eastern Asia is the most populated in the world. More than one half of the world's people

Southern and Eastern Asia is home to people of many different cultures.

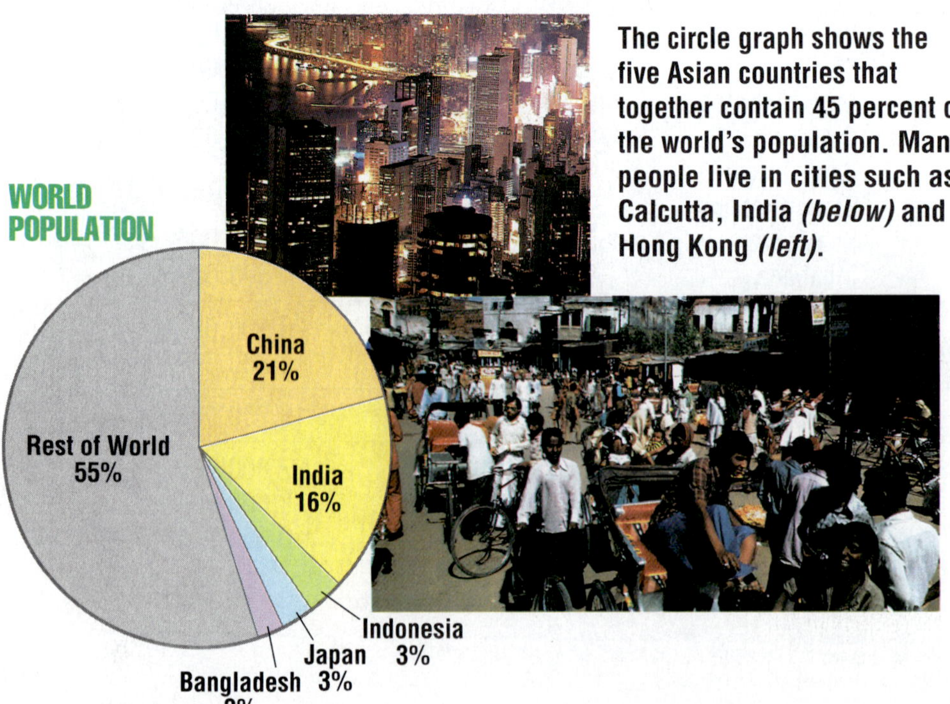

The circle graph shows the five Asian countries that together contain 45 percent of the world's population. Many people live in cities such as Calcutta, India *(below)* and Hong Kong *(left)*.

live here, although the region contains less than one fifth of all the land on the earth. China alone houses over one billion people, or about one fifth of the world's population. India is only about one third the size of the United States, but it contains 859 million people—more than three times the number of people that live in the United States!

As you look at the maps of this region, think about what it would take to meet the basic needs of over one billion people. Judging from the maps of Southern and Eastern Asia, conclude how well equipped this region is to meet the needs and wants of all its people.

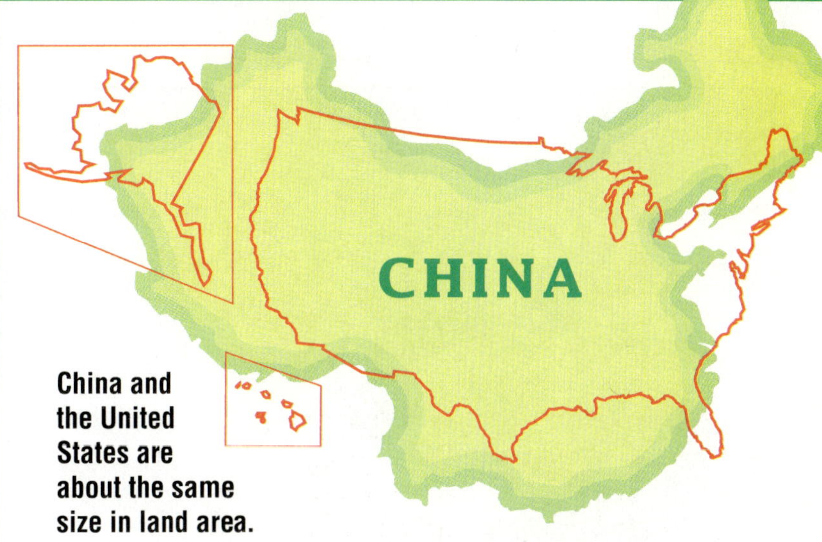

China and the United States are about the same size in land area.

China's Great Wall is 1,500 miles (2,200 km) long. It is the only human-made object that can be seen from space.

People in Nepal raise crops and animals in the awesome shadow of Mount Everest, the world's tallest mountain.

Farmers in Southern Asia depend on summer rains to water their crops.

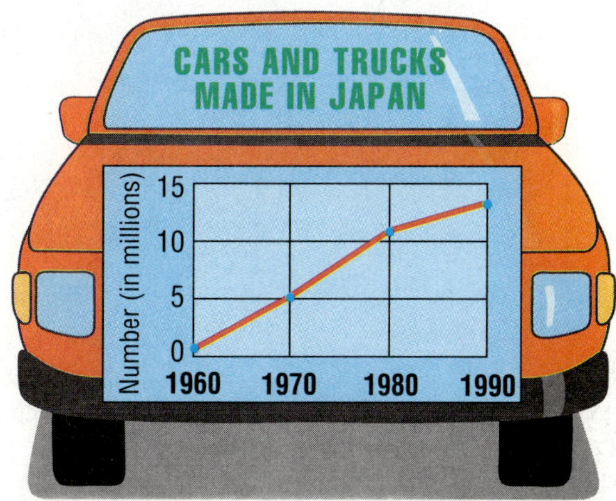

Over the past 30 years, Japan has become a world leader in the production of cars and trucks. According to the graph, between what years did Japan's production grow the most?

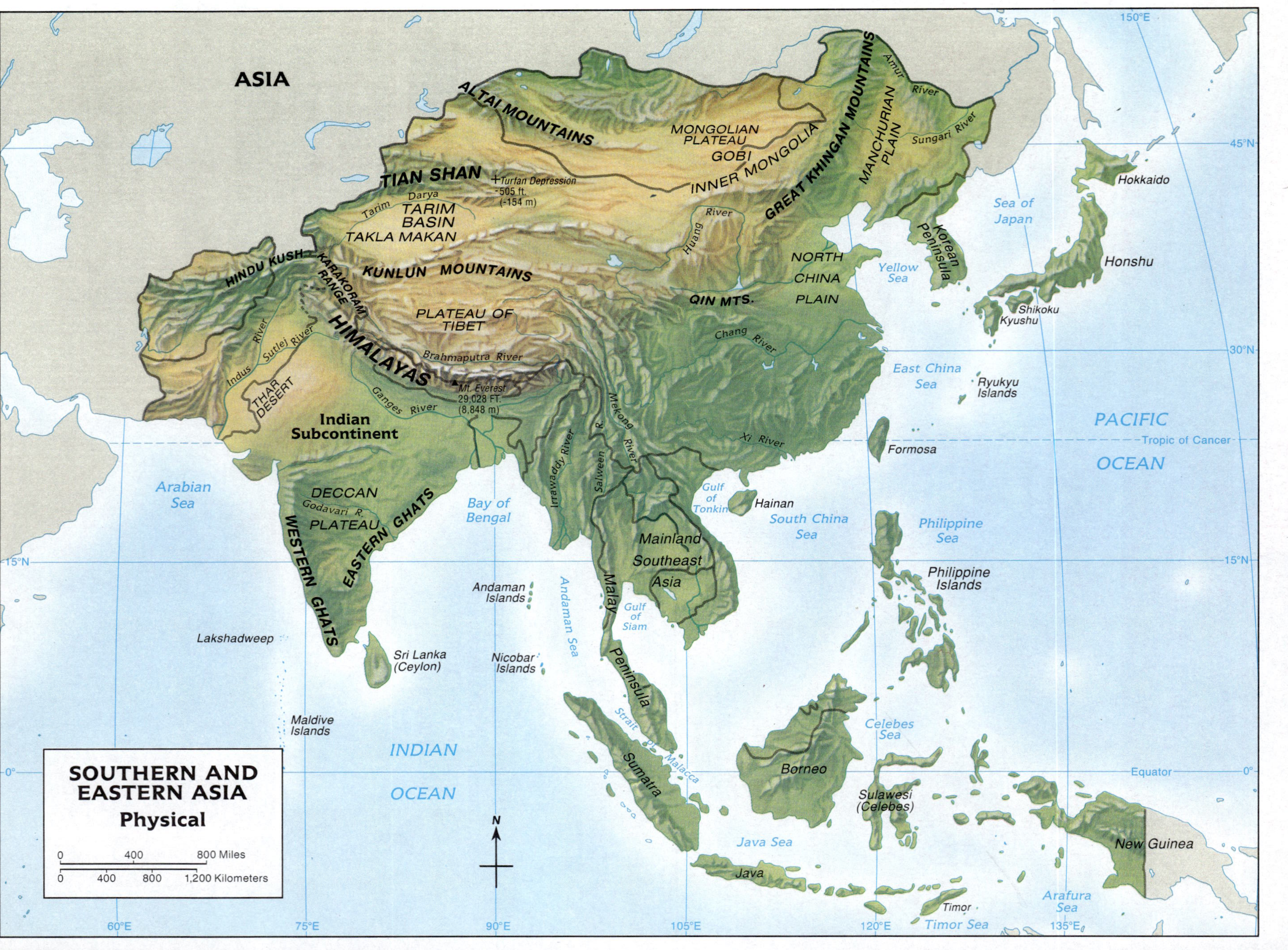

SOUTHERN AND EASTERN ASIA
Physical
0 400 800 Miles
0 400 800 1,200 Kilometers
ASIA
ALTAI MOUNTAINS
MONGOLIAN PLATEAU
GOBI
INNER MONGOLIA
GREAT KHINGAN MOUNTAINS
MANCHURIAN PLAIN
Amur River
Sungari River
TIAN SHAN
Turfan Depression -505 ft. (-154 m)
Tarim Darya
TARIM BASIN
TAKLA MAKAN
HINDU KUSH
KARAKORAM RANGE
KUNLUN MOUNTAINS
PLATEAU OF TIBET
HIMALAYAS
Brahmaputra River
Mt. Everest 29,028 FT. (8,848 m)
Huang River
NORTH CHINA PLAIN
QIN MTS.
Chang River
Xi River
Mekong River
Salween R.
Irrawaddy River
Indus River
Sutlej River
THAR DESERT
Ganges River
Indian Subcontinent
DECCAN PLATEAU
Godavari R.
WESTERN GHATS
EASTERN GHATS
Arabian Sea
Bay of Bengal
Lakshadweep
Sri Lanka (Ceylon)
Maldive Islands
Andaman Islands
Nicobar Islands
Andaman Sea
INDIAN OCEAN
N
Mainland Southeast Asia
Malay Peninsula
Gulf of Siam
Gulf of Tonkin
Hainan
South China Sea
Strait of Malacca
Sumatra
Java
Java Sea
Borneo
Celebes Sea
Sulawesi (Celebes)
Timor
Timor Sea
Arafura Sea
New Guinea
Philippine Islands
Philippine Sea
Formosa
East China Sea
Ryukyu Islands
Yellow Sea
Korean Peninsula
Sea of Japan
Hokkaido
Honshu
Shikoku
Kyushu
PACIFIC OCEAN
Tropic of Cancer
Equator
150°E
45°N
30°N
15°N
0°
60°E
75°E
90°E
105°E
120°E
135°E

SOUTHERN AND EASTERN ASIA
Political
National capital
Other city
0 400 800 Miles
0 400 800 1,200 Kilometers
ASIA
MONGOLIA
Ulaanbaatar
CHINA
MANCHURIA
Harbin
Changchun
Shenyang
Beijing
Tianjin
Jinan
Xi'an
Lanzhou
Huang River
Chang River
Nanjing
Shanghai
Wuhan
Changsha
Chongqing
Chengdu
Kunming
Guangzhou
HONG KONG (U.K.)
MACAU (PORT.)
Amur River
SINKIANG
Urumqi
TIBET
Lhasa
Salween R.
Mekong River
Brahmaputra River
NORTH KOREA
Pyongyang
SOUTH KOREA
Seoul
JAPAN
Tokyo
Nagoya
Kyoto
Nagasaki
Sapporo
Sea of Japan
RYUKYU ISLANDS (JAPAN)
East China Sea
TAIWAN
Taipei
PACIFIC OCEAN
Tropic of Cancer
PHILIPPINES
Manila
Quezon City
Davao
South China Sea
VIETNAM
Hanoi
Hue
Ho Chi Minh City
LAOS
Vientiane
CAMBODIA
Phnom Penh
THAILAND
Bangkok
Moulmein
MYANMAR (BURMA)
Mandalay
Yangon (Rangoon)
Irrawaddy R.
BHUTAN
Thimphu
BANGLADESH
Dhaka
NEPAL
Kathmandu
INDIA
New Delhi
Agra
Patna
Calcutta
Jabalpur
Nagpur
Ahmadabad
Hyderabad
Bombay
Bangalore
Madras
Ganges River
JAMMU AND KASHMIR
PAKISTAN
Islamabad
Lahore
Hyderabad
Karachi
Indus River
AFGHANISTAN
Kabul
Herat
Kandahar
Arabian Sea
Bay of Bengal
ANDAMAN ISLANDS (INDIA)
NICOBAR ISLANDS (INDIA)
SRI LANKA
Colombo
MALDIVES
Male
INDIAN OCEAN
MALAYSIA
Kuala Lumpur
SINGAPORE
Singapore
BRUNEI
Bandar Seri Begawan
INDONESIA
Jakarta
Yogyakarta
Surabaya
Padang
Palembang
Manado
Jayapura
IRIAN JAYA
Arafura Sea
Timor Sea
Equator
N
45°N
30°N
15°N
0°
60°E
75°E
90°E
105°E
120°E
135°E
150°E

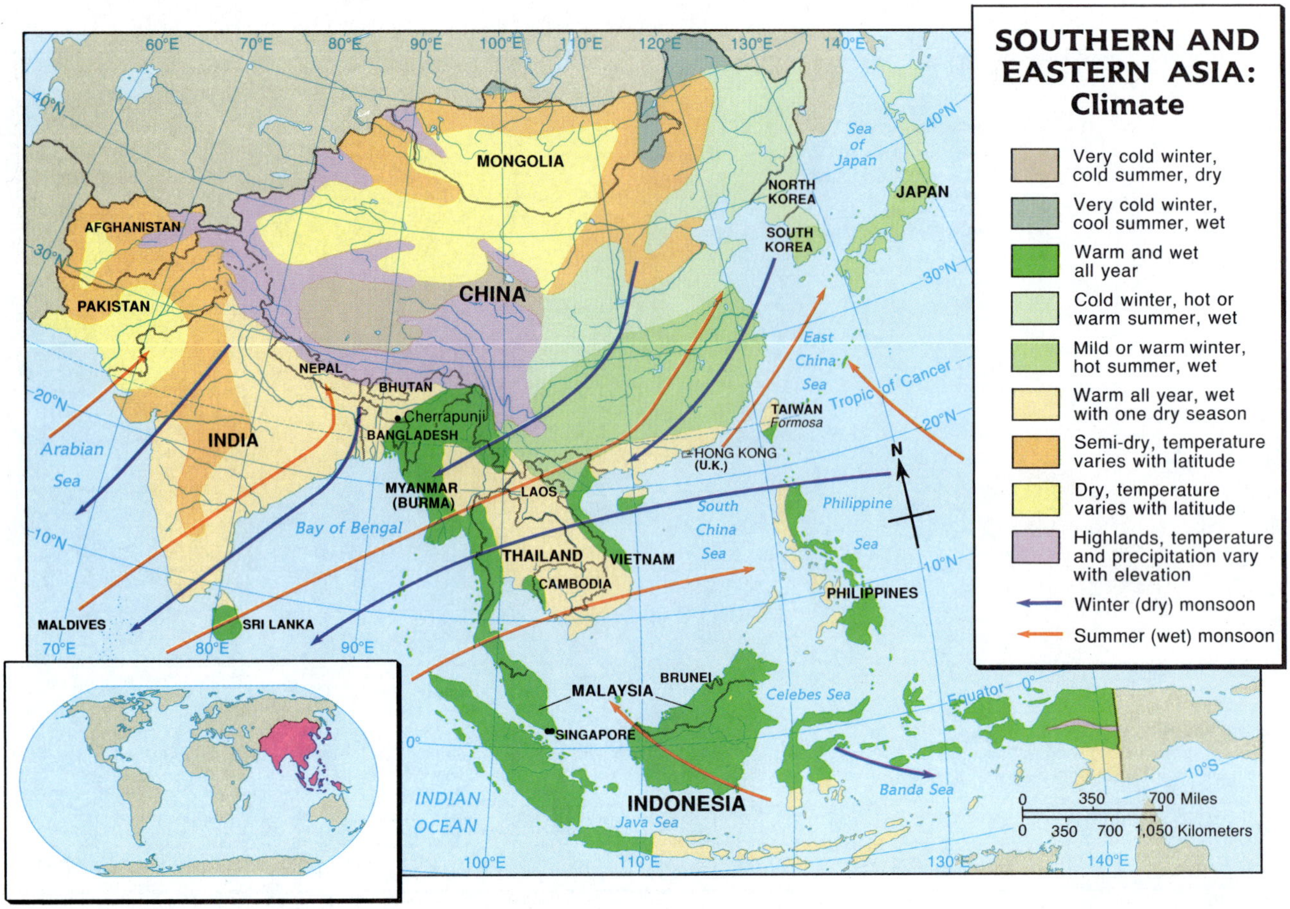
SOUTHERN AND EASTERN ASIA: Climate
Very cold winter, cold summer, dry
Very cold winter, cool summer, wet
Warm and wet all year
Cold winter, hot or warm summer, wet
Mild or warm winter, hot summer, wet
Warm all year, wet with one dry season
Semi-dry, temperature varies with latitude
Dry, temperature varies with latitude
Highlands, temperature and precipitation vary with elevation
Winter (dry) monsoon
Summer (wet) monsoon
MONGOLIA
CHINA
AFGHANISTAN
PAKISTAN
NEPAL
BHUTAN
INDIA
Cherrapunji
BANGLADESH
MYANMAR (BURMA)
LAOS
THAILAND
VIETNAM
CAMBODIA
NORTH KOREA
SOUTH KOREA
JAPAN
TAIWAN Formosa
HONG KONG (U.K.)
PHILIPPINES
MALDIVES
SRI LANKA
MALAYSIA
BRUNEI
SINGAPORE
INDONESIA
Sea of Japan
East China Sea
South China Sea
Philippine Sea
Celebes Sea
Banda Sea
Java Sea
Arabian Sea
Bay of Bengal
INDIAN OCEAN
Tropic of Cancer
Equator
N
0 350 700 Miles
0 350 700 1,050 Kilometers
60°E
70°E
80°E
90°E
100°E
110°E
120°E
130°E
140°E
40°N
30°N
20°N
10°N
0°
10°S

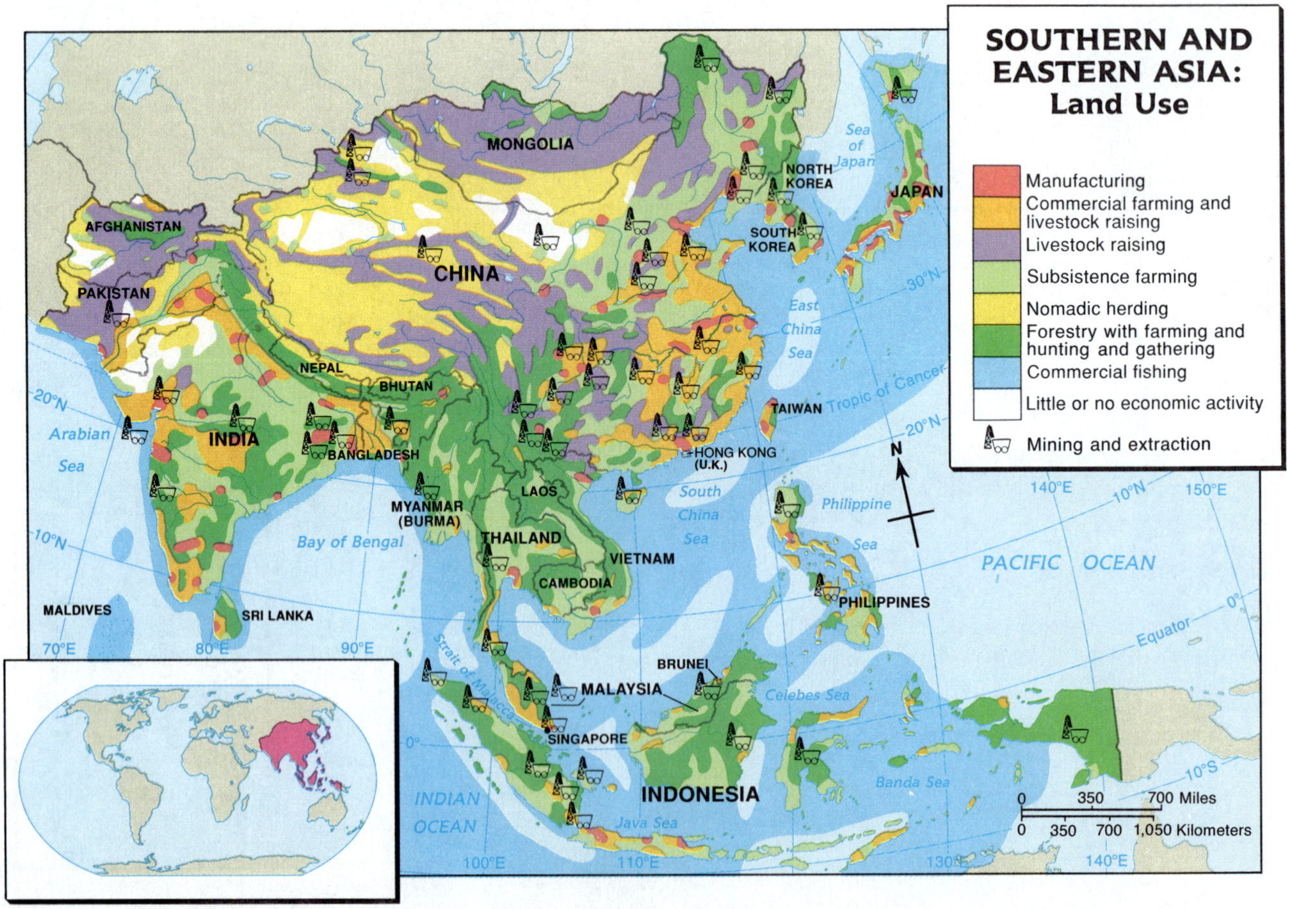
SOUTHERN AND EASTERN ASIA: Land Use
Manufacturing
Commercial farming and livestock raising
Livestock raising
Subsistence farming
Nomadic herding
Forestry with farming and hunting and gathering
Commercial fishing
Little or no economic activity
Mining and extraction
MONGOLIA
CHINA
AFGHANISTAN
PAKISTAN
NEPAL
BHUTAN
INDIA
BANGLADESH
MYANMAR (BURMA)
LAOS
THAILAND
VIETNAM
CAMBODIA
NORTH KOREA
SOUTH KOREA
JAPAN
TAIWAN
HONG KONG (U.K.)
PHILIPPINES
MALDIVES
SRI LANKA
MALAYSIA
BRUNEI
SINGAPORE
INDONESIA
Sea of Japan
East China Sea
South China Sea
Philippine Sea
Celebes Sea
Banda Sea
Java Sea
Arabian Sea
Bay of Bengal
Strait of Malacca
INDIAN OCEAN
PACIFIC OCEAN
Tropic of Cancer
Equator
N
0 350 700 Miles
0 350 700 1,050 Kilometers
70°E
80°E
90°E
100°E
110°E
130°E
140°E
150°E
30°N
20°N
10°N
0°
10°S

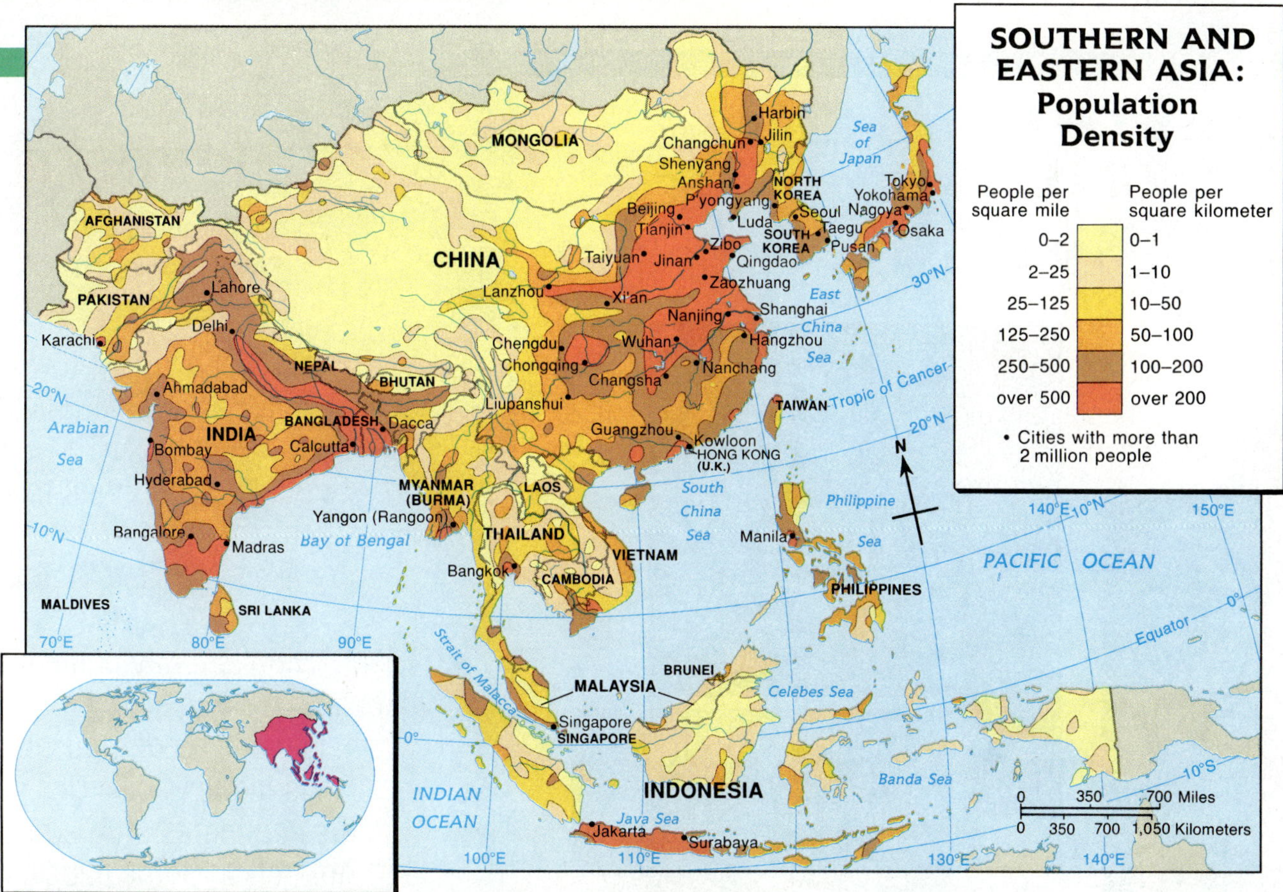

SOUTHERN AND EASTERN ASIA

Country	Capital	Area in sq mi (sq km)	Population
Afghanistan	Kabul	251,773 (647,500)	16,600,000
Bangladesh	Dhaka	55,599 (144,000)	116,600,000
Bhutan	Thimphu	18,147 (47,000)	700,000
Brunei	Bandar Seri Begawan	2,228 (5,770)	300,000
Cambodia	Phnom Penh	69,900 (181,040)	7,100,000
China	Beijing	3,705,396 (9,596,960)	1,151,300,000
India	New Delhi	1,269,342 (3,287,590)	859,200,000
Indonesia	Jakarta	741,098 (1,919,440)	181,400,000
Japan	Tokyo	143,749 (372,310)	123,800,000
Korea, North	Pyongyang	46,541 (120,540)	21,800,000
Korea, South	Seoul	38,023 (98,480)	43,200,000
Laos	Vientiane	91,429 (236,800)	4,100,000
Malaysia	Kuala Lumpur	127,317 (329,750)	18,300,000
Maldives	Malé	116 (300)	200,000
Mongolia	Ulaanbaatar	604,248 (1,565,000)	2,200,000
Myanmar (Burma)	Yangon (Rangoon)	261,217 (676,550)	42,100,000
Nepal	Kathmandu	54,363 (140,800)	19,600,000
Pakistan	Islamabad	310,402 (803,940)	117,500,000
Philippines	Manila	115,830 (300,000)	62,300,000
Singapore	Singapore	224 (580)	2,800,000
Sri Lanka	Colombo	25,332 (65,610)	17,400,000
Taiwan	Taipei	13,892 (35,980)	20,500,000
Thailand	Bangkok	198,456 (514,000)	58,800,000
Vietnam	Hanoi	127,243 (329,560)	67,600,000

THE PACIFIC

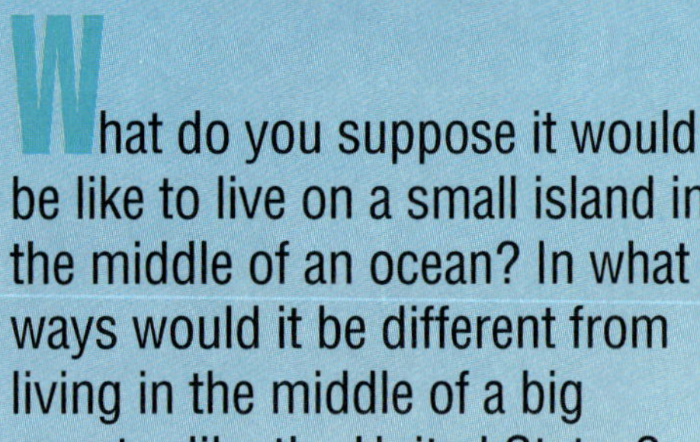

What do you suppose it would be like to live on a small island in the middle of an ocean? In what ways would it be different from living in the middle of a big country like the United States?

Island living is a way of life for people in the Pacific region, which is made up of thousands of islands in the Pacific Ocean and the continents of Australia and Antarctica. Some people live on tiny islands that are hundreds of miles away from each other. Many others live on the con-

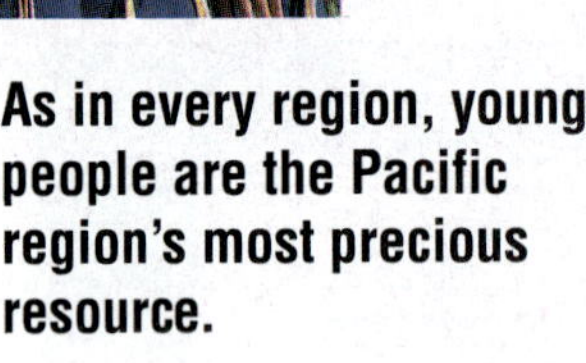

As in every region, young people are the Pacific region's most precious resource.

WORLD'S FRESHWATER SUPPLY

Other 30%

Antarctica 70%

According to the graph, what percentage of the world's freshwater supply is located in Antarctica?

Antarctica's icy landscape is home to penguins—but not polar bears. As the drawing shows, polar bears live only near the North Pole.

tinent of Australia, which is hardly a tiny island but is still isolated by miles of ocean from its nearest neighbor.

The mighty Pacific Ocean is the tie that binds the people and lands of this region together. As you look at the maps in this section, think about how the Pacific Ocean helps to provide the basic needs of the people in this region. Then think about how it limits the way people in the Pacific region live.

Many Australians live on isolated farms and ranches. Some young people even "go to school" by radio because they live too far away from the nearest school.

→ NEW ZEALAND 1,600 mi
↑ HONG KONG 4,300 mi
↗ LOS ANGELES 7,600 mi
↖ LONDON 10,200 mi

Australia

This island, like many in the Pacific region, is made of coral.

In New Zealand, sheep outnumber people by 20 to 1.

Ayers Rock towers above the desert-like Australian outback.

The Sydney Opera House is one of the most famous landmarks in Australia.

The Pacific region is located within the "Ring of Fire," the volcanic chain that rims the Pacific Ocean. Most of the world's volcanoes are found along this chain.

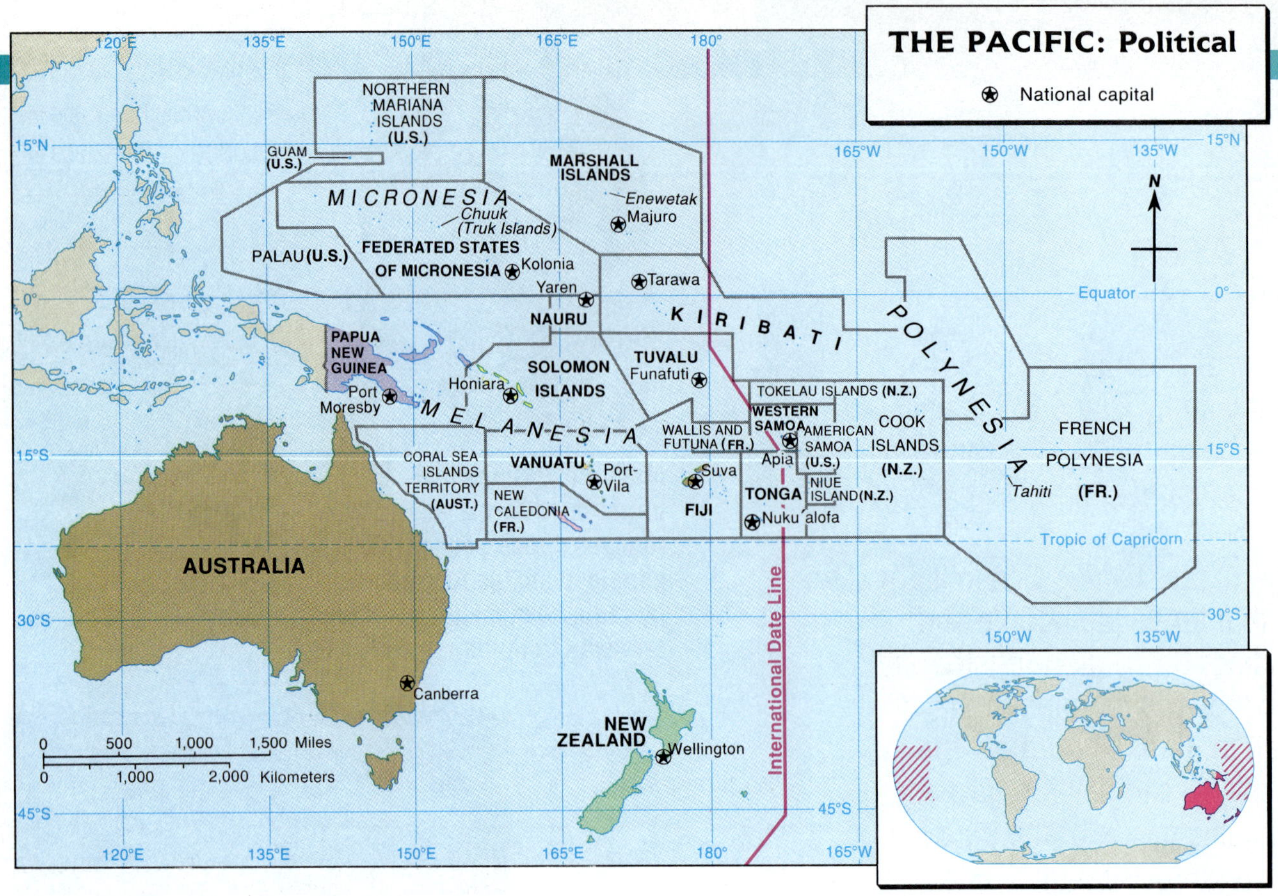

THE PACIFIC

Country	Capital	Area in sq mi (sq km)	Population
Australia	Canberra	2,967,900 (7,686,850)	17,500,000
Fiji	Suva	7,054 (18,270)	700,000
Kiribati	Tarawa	277 (717)	71,000
Marshall Islands	Majuro	70 (113)	43,000
Nauru	Yaren	8 (20)	8,100
New Zealand	Wellington	103,738 (268,680)	3,500,000
Papua New Guinea	Port Moresby	178,259 (461,690)	3,900,000
Solomon Islands	Honiara	10,985 (28,450)	300,000
Tonga	Nuku'alofa	270 (700)	102,000
Tuvalu	Funafuti	10 (26)	9,000
Vanuatu	Port-Vila	5,699 (14,760)	200,000
Western Samoa	Apia	1,104 (2,860)	200,000

AUSTRALIA AND NEW ZEALAND
Physical
0 250 500 750 Miles
0 250 500 750 1,000 Kilometers
INDONESIA
PAPUA NEW GUINEA
SOLOMON ISLANDS
PACIFIC OCEAN
INDIAN OCEAN
Arafura Sea
Timor Sea
Torres Strait
Coral Sea
Tasman Sea
Melville Island
Cape York
Cape Londonderry
Joseph Bonaparte Gulf
Groote Eylandt
Gulf of Carpentaria
Daly River
Victoria River
Ord River
KIMBERLY PLATEAU
KING LEOPOLD RANGES
Fitzroy River
GREAT SANDY DESERT
CAPE YORK PENINSULA
Mitchell River
Great Barrier Reef
BARKLY TABLELAND
Flinders River
GREAT DIVIDING RANGE
Northwest Cape
Ashburton River
Gascoyne River
Murchison River
Lake Mackay
Lake Disappointment
GIBSON DESERT
Lake Hopkins
MACDONNELL RANGES
Lake Amadeus
SIMPSON DESERT
GREAT ARTESIAN BASIN
NEW CALEDONIA (FR.)
Tropic of Capricorn
Lake Carnegie
AUSTRALIA
Warburton River
Cooper Creek
Lake Eyre
Lake Barlee
GREAT VICTORIAN DESERT
NULLABOR PLAIN
Lake Torrens
Lake Gairdner
Lake Cowan
Great Australian Bight
EYRE PENINSULA
Spencer Gulf
Kangaroo Island
Darling River
Lachlan River
Murrumbidgee River
Murray River
Mt. Kosciusko 7,330 ft. (2,228m)
Cape Howe
Norfolk Island
Cape Leeuwin
King Island
Bass Strait
Flinders Island
Tasmania
Southwest Cape
NEW ZEALAND
North Cape
North Island
Bay of Plenty
Lake Taupo
Cape Farewell
Cook Strait
Mt. Cook 12,350 ft. (3,742m)
SOUTHERN ALPS
South Island
Canterbury Bight
Foveaux Strait
Stewart Island
N
120°E
135°E
150°E
165°E
180°
15°S
30°S
45°S

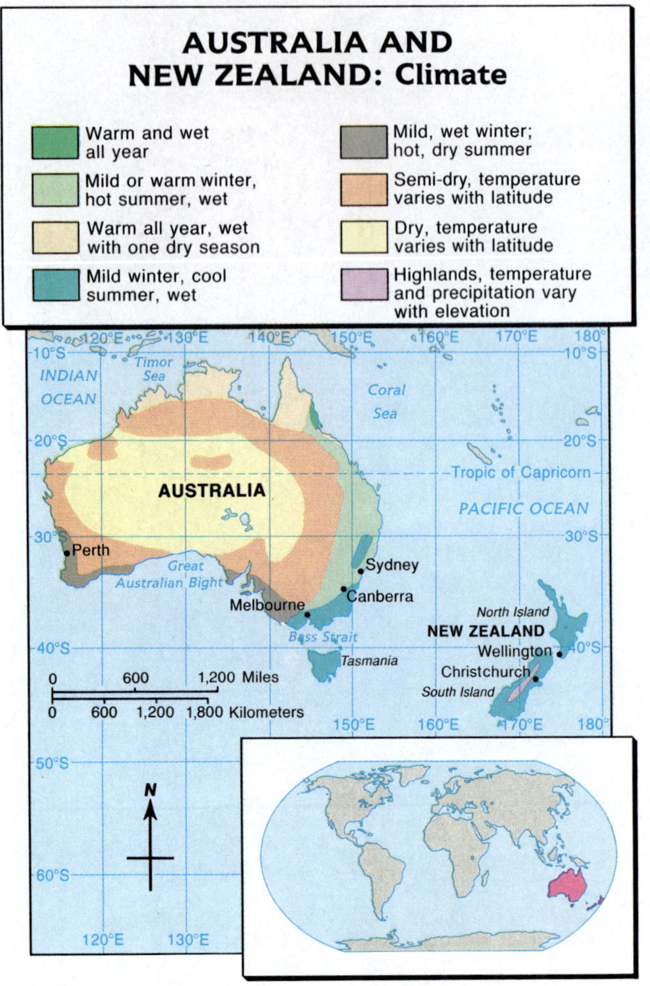
AUSTRALIA AND
NEW ZEALAND: Climate
Warm and wet all year
Mild or warm winter, hot summer, wet
Warm all year, wet with one dry season
Mild winter, cool summer, wet
Mild, wet winter; hot, dry summer
Semi-dry, temperature varies with latitude
Dry, temperature varies with latitude
Highlands, temperature and precipitation vary with elevation
INDIAN OCEAN
Timor Sea
Coral Sea
Tropic of Capricorn
PACIFIC OCEAN
AUSTRALIA
Perth
Great Australian Bight
Sydney
Canberra
Melbourne
Bass Strait
Tasmania
North Island
NEW ZEALAND
Wellington
Christchurch
South Island
0 600 1,200 Miles
0 600 1,200 1,800 Kilometers
N

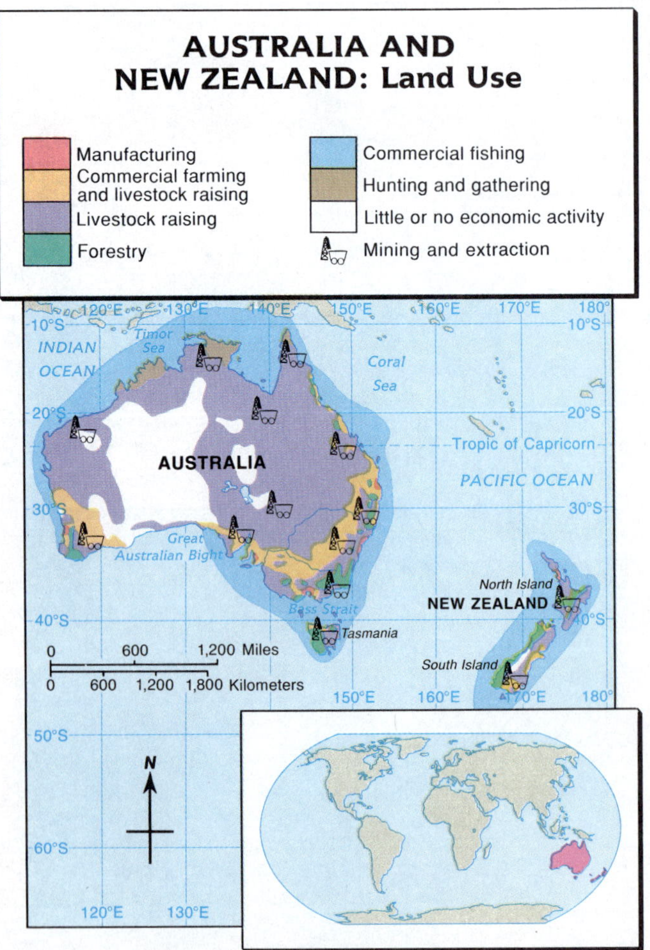
AUSTRALIA AND
NEW ZEALAND: Land Use
Manufacturing
Commercial farming and livestock raising
Livestock raising
Forestry
Commercial fishing
Hunting and gathering
Little or no economic activity
Mining and extraction
INDIAN OCEAN
Timor Sea
Coral Sea
Tropic of Capricorn
PACIFIC OCEAN
AUSTRALIA
Great Australian Bight
Bass Strait
Tasmania
North Island
NEW ZEALAND
South Island
0 600 1,200 Miles
0 600 1,200 1,800 Kilometers
N

AUSTRALIA AND NEW ZEALAND: Population Density

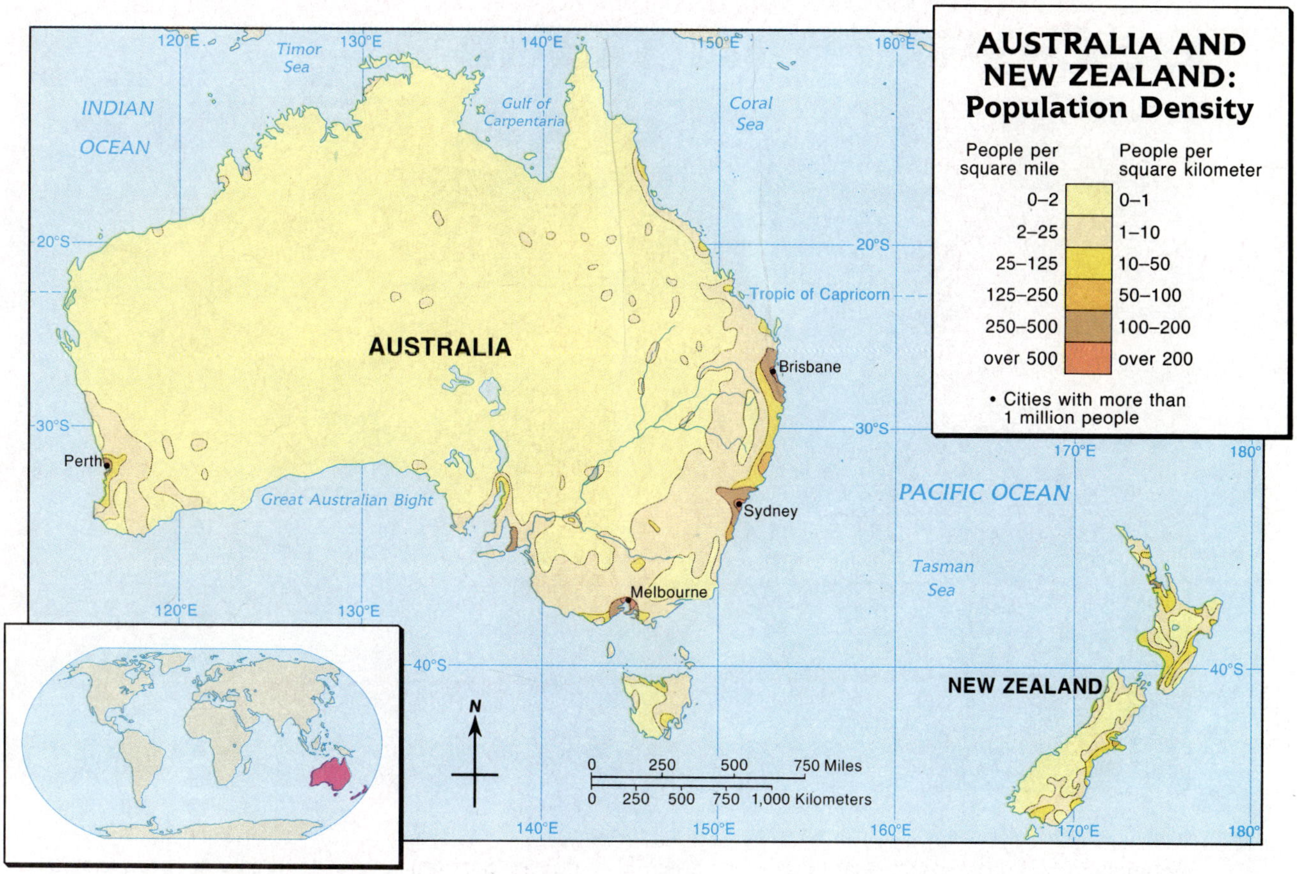

People per square mile	People per square kilometer
0–2	0–1
2–25	1–10
25–125	10–50
125–250	50–100
250–500	100–200
over 500	over 200

• Cities with more than 1 million people

ANTARCTICA: Physical

▲ Tallest mountain

0 500 1,000 Miles
0 500 1,000 1,500 Kilometers

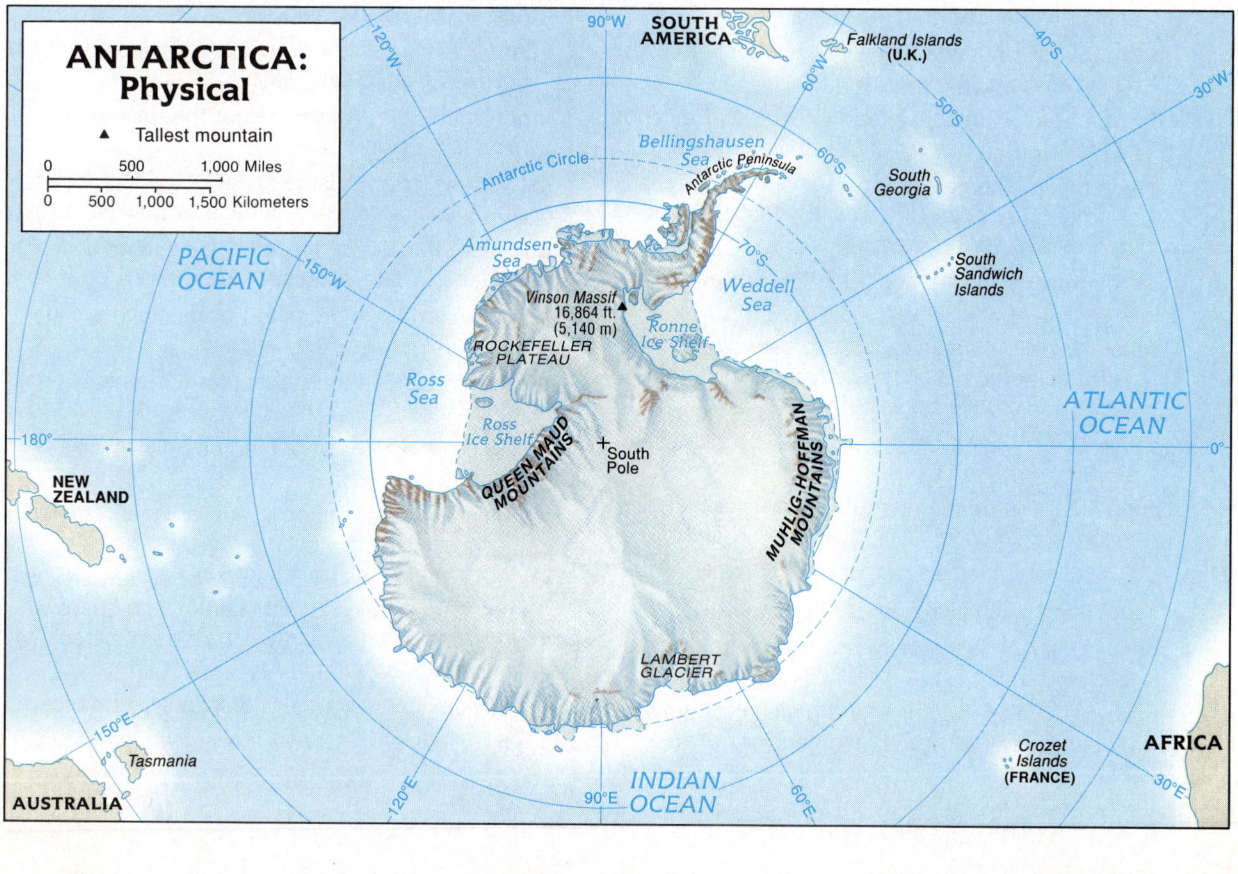

DICTIONARY OF GEOGRAPHIC TERMS

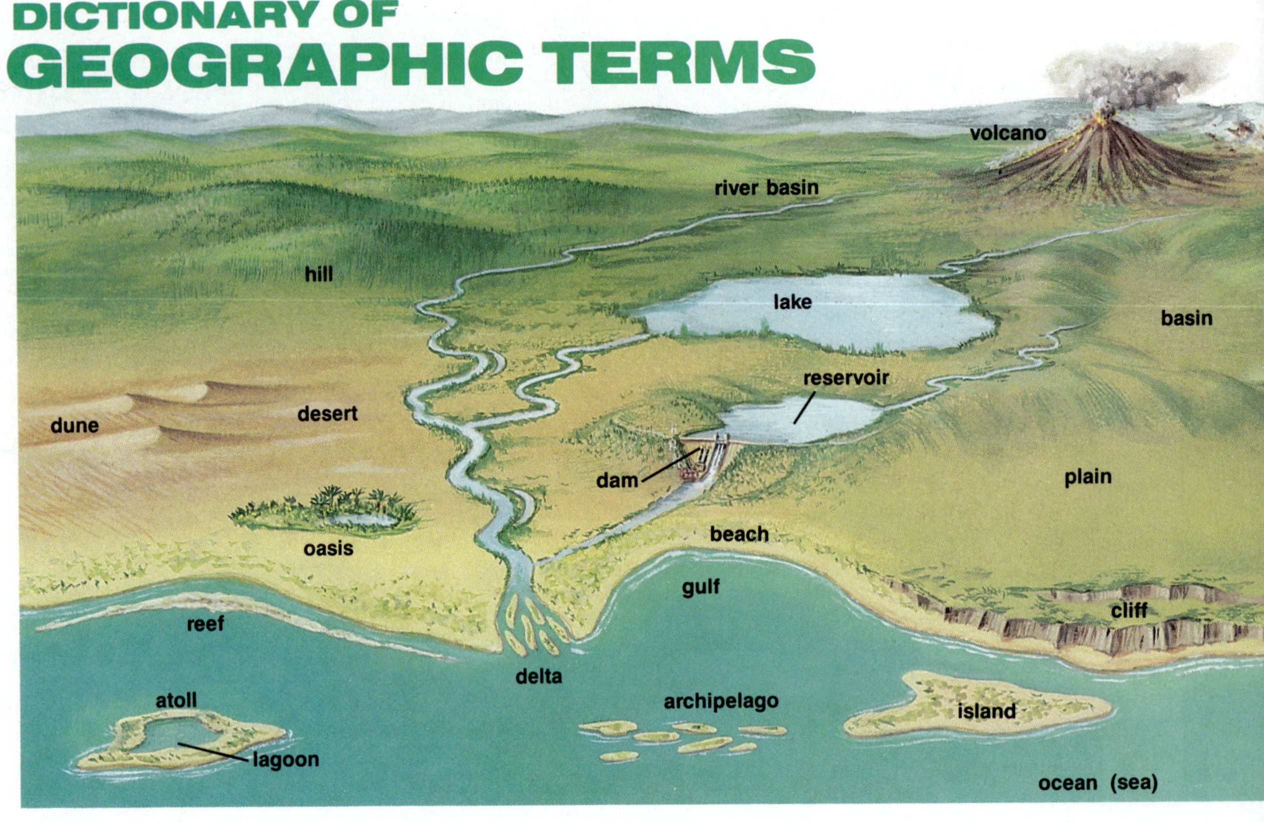

archipelago (är kə pel′ ə gō) A large group or chain of islands.

atoll (āt′ ôl) A ring-shaped coral island or string of islands, surrounding a lagoon.

basin (bā′ sin) An area of low-lying land surrounded by higher land. *See also* **river basin**.

bay (bā) Part of an ocean, sea, or lake, that extends into the land. A bay is usually smaller than a gulf.

beach (bēch) The gently sloping shore of an ocean or other body of water, especially that part covered by sand or pebbles.

butte (būt) A small, flat-topped hill. A butte is smaller than a plateau or a mesa.

canal (kə nal′) A waterway built to carry water for navigation or irrigation. Navigation canals usually connect two other bodies of water.

canyon (kan′ yən) A deep, narrow valley with steep sides.

cape (kāp) A projecting part of a coastline that extends into an ocean, sea, gulf, bay, or lake.

cliff (klif) A high, steep face of rock or earth.

coast (kōst) Land along an ocean or sea.

dam (dam) A wall built across a river to hold back the flowing water.

delta (del′ tə) Land formed at the mouth of a river by deposits of silt, sand, and pebbles.

desert (dez′ ərt) A very dry area where few plants grow.

dune (dün) A mound, hill, or ridge of sand that is heaped up by the wind.

fjord (fyôrd) A deep, narrow inlet of the sea between high, steep cliffs.

foothills (fu̇t′ hilz) A hilly area at the base of a mountain range.

glacier (glā′ shər) A large sheet of ice that moves slowly over some land surface or down a valley.

gulf (gulf) Part of an ocean or sea that extends into the land. A gulf is usually larger than a bay.

harbor (här′ bər) A protected place along a shore where ships can safely anchor.

hill (hil) A rounded, raised landform, not as high as a mountain.

island (ī′ lənd) A body of land completely surrounded by water.

isthmus (is′ məs) A narrow strip of land bordered by water, that connects two larger bodies of land.

lagoon (lə gün′) A shallow body of water partly or completely enclosed within an atoll; a shallow body of sea water partly cut off from the sea by a narrow strip of land.

lake (lāk) A body of water completely surrounded by land.

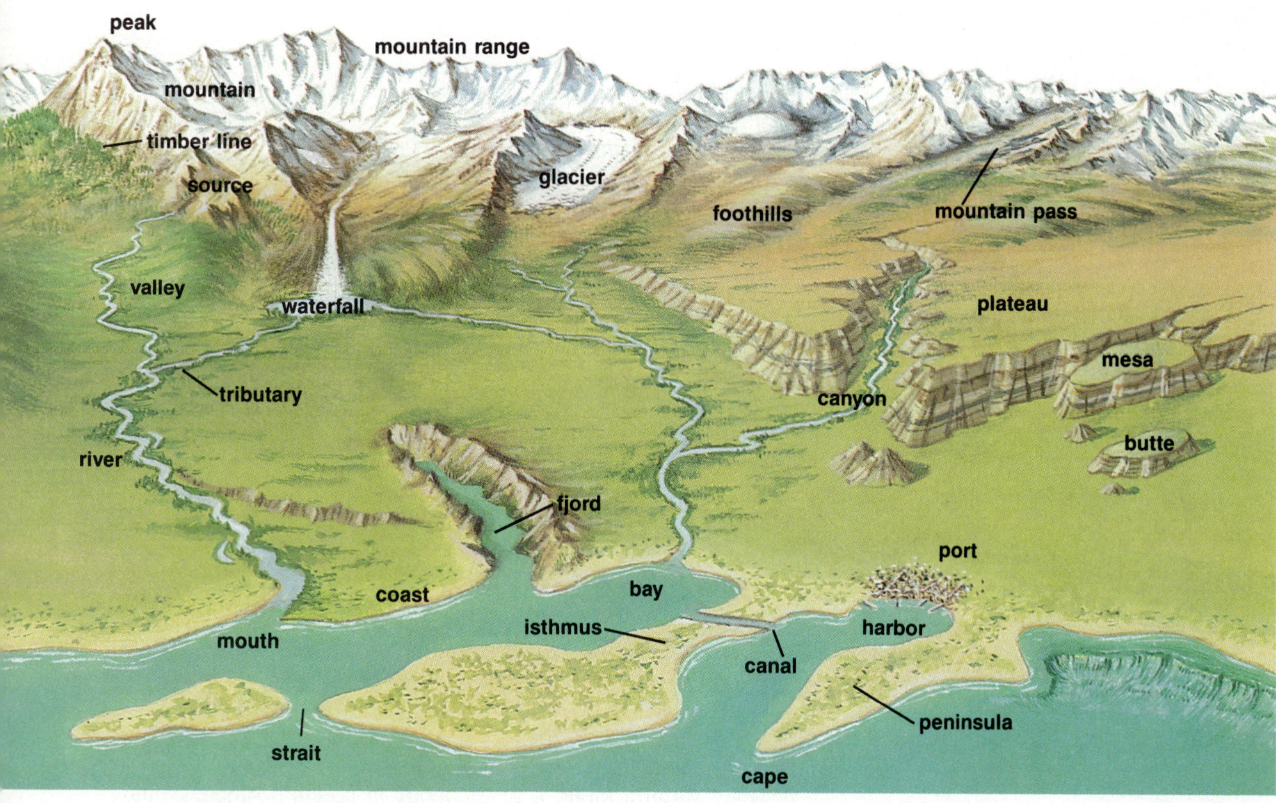

mesa (mā′ sə) A high, flat landform rising steeply above the surrounding land. A mesa is smaller than a plateau and larger than a butte.

mountain (mount′ ən) A high, rounded or pointed landform with steep sides, higher than a hill.

mountain pass (mount′ ən pas) An opening or gap through a mountain range.

mountain range (mount′ ən rānj) A row or chain of mountains.

mouth (mouth) The place where a river empties into another body of water.

oasis (ō ā′ sis) A place in the desert made fertile by a steady supply of water.

ocean (ō′ shən) One of the earth's four largest bodies of water. The four oceans are really a single connected body of salt water that covers about three fourths of the earth's surface.

peak (pēk) The pointed top of a mountain or hill.

peninsula (pə nin′ sə lə) A body of land nearly surrounded by water.

plain (plān) A large area of flat or nearly flat land.

plateau (pla tō′) A high, flat landform that rises steeply above the surrounding land. A plateau is larger than a mesa and a butte.

port (pôrt) A place where ships load and unload goods.

reef (rēf) A ridge of sand, rock, or coral that lies at or near the surface of a sea.

reservoir (rez′ ər vwär) A natural or artificial lake used to store water.

river (riv′ ər) A large stream of water that flows across the land and usually empties into a lake, ocean, or other river.

river basin (riv′ ər bās′ in) All the land drained by a river and its tributaries.

sea (sē) A large body of water partly or entirely surrounded by land; another word for *ocean.*

source (sôrs) The place where a river or stream begins.

strait (strāt) A narrow waterway or channel connecting two larger bodies of water.

timber line (tim′ bər līn) An imaginary line on mountains, above which trees do not grow.

tributary (trib′ yə târ ē) A river or stream that flows into a larger river or stream.

valley (val′ ē) An area of low land between hills or mountains.

volcano (vol kā′ nō) An opening in the earth through which lava, rock, gases, and ash are forced out.

waterfall (wô′ tər fôl) A flow of water falling from a high place to a lower place.

GAZETTEER

This Gazetteer is a geographical dictionary that will help you to pronounce and locate the places shown in this Atlas. Latitude and longitude are given for cities and some other places. The page number tells you where each place appears on a regional map for the first time.

PRONUNCIATION KEY

a	cap	êr	clear	oi	coin	ü	moon
ā	cake	hw	where	ôr	fork	ū	cute
ä	father	i	bib	ou	cow	ûr	term
är	car	ī	kite	sh	show	ə	about, taken pencil, apron, helpful
âr	dare	ng	song	th	thin	ər	letter, dollar, doctor
ch	chain	o	top	th̲	those		
e	hen	ō	rope	u	sun		
ē	me	ô	saw	u̇	book		

A

Abidjan (ab i jän′) The capital of Côte d'Ivoire; 5°N, 4°W. (p. 57)

Abu Dhabi (ä bü dä′ bē) The capital of the United Arab Emirates; 25°N, 55°E. (p. 51)

Abuja (ä bu′ jə) The capital of Nigeria; 6°N, 3°E. (p. 57)

Accra (ə krä′) The capital and largest city of Ghana; 5°N, 1°W. (p. 57)

Addis Ababa (ad′ is ab′ ə bə) The capital and largest city of Ethiopia; 9°N, 38°E. (p. 57)

Adelaide (ad′ ə lād) A city in southern Australia; 138°E, 35°S. (p. 71)

Afghanistan (af gan′ ə stan) A country in south-central Asia. Capital, Kabul. (p. 65)

Africa (af′ ri kə) The world's second-largest continent. It lies between the Atlantic and Indian oceans. (p. 3)

Ahaggar Mountains (ə häg′ ər moun′ tənz) A mountainous region in the central Sahara in Africa. (p. 50)

Ahmadabad (ä mə də bäd′) A city in west-central India; 26°N, 73°E. (p. 65)

Alabama (al ə bam′ ə) A state in the southeastern United States. Capital, Montgomery. (p. 15)

Alaska (ə las′ kə) The largest state of the United States, on the extreme northwestern peninsula of North America. Capital, Juneau. (p. 15)

Alaska Range (ə las′ kə rānj) A mountain range stretching across southern Alaska. (p. 14)

Albania (al bā′ nē ə) A country in southeastern Europe, on the Balkan Peninsula. Capital, Tiranë. (p. 43)

Albany (ôl′ bə nē) The capital of New York; 42°N, 70°W. (p. 15)

Alexandria (al ig zan′ drē ə) A port city in Egypt; 2°N, 30°E. (p. 51)

Algeria (al jîr′ ē ə) A country in northern Africa, on the Mediterranean Sea. Capital, Algiers. (p. 51)

Algiers (al jîrz′) The capital of Algeria; 36°N, 7°W. (p. 51)

Allegheny River (al i gā′ nē riv′ ər) A river in western Pennsylvania and in southwestern New York. Length, 325 miles (523 km). (p. 22)

Alma-Ata (al′ mə a′ tä) The capital of Kazakhstan; 44°N, 77°E. (p. 43)

Alps (alps) A major European mountain system, extending in an arc from the Mediterranean coast east to the Balkan Peninsula. (p. 42)

Altai Mountains (al′ tī moun′ tənz) A mountain range in Asia, extending from the south-central part of Russia east into western Mongolia. (p. 42)

Amazon River (am′ ə zon riv′ ər) The longest river in South America and the second-longest river in the world. Length, 4,000 miles (6,400 km). (p. 34)

American Samoa (ə mer′ i kən sə mō′ ə) An island group in the Pacific Ocean, a territory of the United States. Capital, Pago Pago. (p. 71)

Amman (ä män′) The capital of Jordan; 31°N, 35°E. (p. 51)

Amsterdam (am′ stər dam) The capital and largest city of the Netherlands; 52°N, 4°E. (p. 43)

Amu Darya (ä mü där′ yə) A river in central Asia, flowing into the Aral Sea. Length, 1,578 miles (2,545 km). (p. 42)

Amur River (ä mu̇r′ riv′ ər) A river in northeastern Asia, forming part of the boundary between Russia and China. Length, 2,744 miles (4,390 km). (p. 42)

Anadyr' Range (än ə dir′ rānj) An extension of the Kolyma Mountains, near the Arctic Circle in Russia. (p. 42)

Andaman Islands (an′ də mən ī′ ləndz) A group of islands located in the Andaman Sea. (p. 65)
Andaman Sea (an′ də mən sē) The northeastern part of the Indian Ocean, lying between India and the Malay Peninsula. (p. 64)
Andes Mountains (an′ dēz moun′ tənz) The longest mountain chain in the world, stretching along the west coast of South America. (p. 34)
Andorra (an dôr′ ə) A country in southwestern Europe, between France and Spain. Capital, Andorra la Vella. (p. 43)
Angola (ang gō′ lə) A country on the west coast of southern Africa. Capital, Luanda. (p. 57)
Ankara (ang′ kər ə) The capital of Turkey; 39°N, 32°E. (p. 51)
Annapolis (ə nap′ ə lis) The capital of Maryland; 39°N, 76°W. (p. 15)
Antananarivo (än tə nä nə rē′ vō) The capital of Madagascar; 18°S, 47°E. (p. 57)
Antarctica (ant ärk′ ti kə) The fifth-largest continent. Ice-covered, it surrounds the South Pole and lies mainly within the Antarctic Circle. (p. 2)
Antarctic Ocean (ant ärk′ tik ō′ shən) A body of water surrounding Antarctica, consisting of the southernmost parts of the Atlantic, Pacific, and Indian oceans. (p. 71)
Antigua and Barbuda (an tē′ gə and bär bü′ də) An island nation of the West Indies. Capital, St. John's. (p. 35)
Apennines (ap′ ə nīnz) A mountain range located in central Italy. (p. 42)
Apia (ä pē′ ə) The capital of Western Samoa; 14°S, 172°W. (p. 71)
Appalachian Mountains (ap ə lā′ chē ən moun′ tənz) Low, rounded mountains that cover much of the eastern United States from Maine to Alabama. (p. 14)
Arabian Peninsula (ə rā′ bē ən pə nin′ sə lə) A large peninsula in southwestern Asia. (p. 50)
Arabian Sea (ə rā′ bē ən sē) The northwestern part of the Indian Ocean. (p. 50)
Arafura Sea (ar ə fùr′ ə sē) A body of water between northern Australia and Indonesia. (p. 70)
Aral Sea (ar′ əl sē) A saltwater lake in the southwestern part of central Asia. (p. 42)
Arctic Ocean (ärk′ tik ō′ shən) The world's smallest ocean. It surrounds the North Pole. (p. 2)
Argentina (är jən tē′ nə) The second-largest country in South America. Capital, Buenos Aires. (p. 35)
Arizona (ar ə zō′ nə) A state in the southwestern United States, bordering Mexico. Capital, Phoenix. (p. 15)
Arkansas (är′ kən sô) A state in the southeastern United States. Capital, Little Rock. (p. 15)
Armenia (är mē′ nē ə) A country in eastern Europe, formerly part of the Soviet Union. Capital, Yerevan. (p. 43)
Aruba (ə rü′ bə) An island in the Caribbean Sea, part of the Netherlands Antilles. (p. 35)
Ashkhabad (ash′ kə bäd) The capital of Turkmenistan; 38°N, 57°E. (p. 43)
Asia (ā′ zhə) The world's largest continent, bounded on the west by Europe, on the east by the Pacific Ocean, and on the south by the Indian Ocean. (p. 3)
Asia Minor (ā′ zhə mī′ nər) A peninsula in western Asia, bordered by the Mediterranean and Black seas. It is also known as Anatolia. (p. 50)
Asunción (ä sün syōn′) The capital and largest city of Paraguay; 25°S, 57°W. (p. 35)
Athens (ath′ ənz) The capital of Greece; 38°N, 24°E. (p. 15)
Atlanta (at lan′ tə) The capital and largest city of Georgia; 33°N, 84°W. (p. 15)
Atlantic Ocean (at lan′ tik ō′ shən) The world's second-largest ocean. It separates North America and South America from Europe and Africa. (p. 2)
Atlas Mountains (at′ ləs moun′ tənz) A mountain range extending along the northwestern coast of Africa. (p. 50)
Augusta (ô gus′ tə) The capital of Maine; 44°N, 69°W. (p. 15)
Austin (ôs′ tin) The capital of Texas; 30°N, 97°W. (p. 15)
Australia (ôs trāl′ yə) The world's smallest continent. Also, a country including the continent of Australia and the island of Tasmania. Capital, Canberra. (p. 71)
Austria (ôs′ trē ə) A country in central Europe. Capital, Vienna. (p. 43)
Azerbaijan (ä zər bī jän′) A country in the Caucasus Mountain region of eastern Europe, formerly part of the Soviet Union. Capital, Baku. (p. 43)
Azores (ə zôrz′) An island group in the northern Atlantic Ocean, west of and belonging to Portugal. (p. 4)

B

Baffin Bay (baf′ in bā) An inlet of the Atlantic Ocean, between Greenland and Baffin Island. (p. 14)
Baghdad (bag′ dad) The capital of Iraq; 33°N, 44°E. (p. 51)
Bahamas (bə hä′ məz) An island country in the West Indies. Capital, Nassau. (p. 35)
Bahrain (bä rān′) An Arab emirate consisting of more than 30 islands in the Persian Gulf. Capital, Manama. (p. 51)
Baku (bä kü′) The capital of Azerbaijan; 40°N, 50°E. (p. 43)
Balearic Islands (bal ē ar′ ik ī′ ləndz) A Spanish island group in the western Mediterranean Sea. (p. 43)
Balkan Peninsula (bôl′ kən pə nin′ sə lə) A large peninsula in southern Europe bounded by the Black, Aegean, and Adriatic seas. (p. 42)
Baltic Sea (bôl′ tik sē) An inland sea in northern Europe. (p. 42)
Bamako (bä mə kō′) The capital of Mali; 12°N, 8°W. (p. 57)
Bandar Seri Begawan (bun′ dər ser′ ē bə gä′ wən) The capital of Brunei; 6°N, 115°E. (p. 65)
Bangkok (bang′ kok) The capital and largest city of Thailand; 13°N, 100°E. (p. 65)
Bangladesh (bang glə desh′) A country located at the northern end of the Bay of Bengal and largely surrounded by India. Capital, Dhaka. (p. 65)
Bangui (bäng′ gē) The capital of the Central African Republic; 5°N, 18°E. (p. 57)
Banjul (bän′ jül) The capital of Gambia; 13°N, 16°W. (p. 57)
Barbados (bär bā′ dōs) An island nation in the Caribbean Sea, the easternmost island of the West Indies. Capital, Bridgetown. (p. 35)

Barents Sea (bar′ ənts sē) An arm of the Arctic Ocean north of Norway and Russia. (p. 42)
Basseterre (bäs târ′) The capital and largest city of St. Kitts and Nevis; 17°N, 62°W. (p. 35)
Baton Rouge (bat′ ən rüzh) The capital of Louisiana; 30°N, 91°W. (p. 15)
Bay of Bengal (bā əv ben′ gôl) The northeastern part of the Indian Ocean. (p. 64)
Bay of Biscay (bā əv bis′ kā) A broad inlet of the northern Atlantic Ocean, between western France and northern Spain. (p. 42)
Beaufort Sea (bō′ fərt sē) An arm of the Arctic, bordering northern Alaska and northwestern Canada. (p. 14)
Beijing (bā′ jing′) The capital of the People's Republic of China. It is also called Peking; 40°N, 116°E. (p. 65)
Beirut (bā rüt′) The capital and largest city of Lebanon; 33°N, 35°E. (p. 51)
Belfast (bel′ fast) The capital and largest city of Northern Ireland; 54°N, 5°W. (p. 43)
Belgium (bel′ jəm) A country in northwestern Europe, on the North Sea. Capital, Brussels. (p. 43)
Belgrade (bel′ grād) The capital and largest city of Yugoslavia; 44°N, 20°E. (p. 43)
Belize (be lēz′) A country on the northeastern coast of Central America. Capital, Belmopan. (p. 35)
Belmopan (bel mō pän′) The capital of Belize; 17°N, 89°W. (p. 35)
Benin (be nēn′) A country in western Africa, on the Gulf of Guinea. Capital, Porto-Novo. (p. 57)
Bering Sea (ber′ ing sē) The northernmost arm of the Pacific Ocean, between Siberia and Alaska. (p. 14)
Bering Strait (ber′ ing strāt) A strait connecting the Bering Sea with the Arctic Ocean. (p. 14)
Bermuda (bər mū′ də) A British island group in the northern Atlantic Ocean. (p. 4)
Bern (bûrn) The capital of Switzerland; 46°N, 7°E. (p. 43)
Bhutan (bü tän′) A country in south-central Asia, in the Himalayas. Capital, Thimphu. (p. 65)
Bishkek (bish′ kek) The capital of Kyrgyzstan; 43°N, 75°E. (p. 43)
Bismarck (biz′ märk) The capital of North Dakota; 46°N, 100°W. (p. 15)
Bissau (bi sou′) The capital of Guinea-Bissau; 11°N, 15°W. (p. 57)
Black Sea (blak sē) An inland sea between Europe and Asia. (p. 42)
Bloemfontein (blüm′ fən tān) The judicial capital of the Republic of South Africa; 29°S, 26°E. (p. 57)
Blue Ridge Mountains (blü rij moun′ tənz) An eastern range of the Appalachian Mountains. (p. 24)
Bogotá (bō′ gə tä) The capital and largest city of Colombia; 5°N, 73°W. (p. 35)
Boise (boi′ zē) The capital of Idaho; 43°N, 116°W. (p. 15)
Bolivia (bə liv′ ē ə) A country in west-central South America. Capitals, La Paz and Sucre. (p. 35)
Bosnia and Herzegovina (boz′ nē ə and hûrt sə gō vē′ nə) A country in southeastern Europe, formerly part of Yugoslavia. Capital, Sarajevo. (p. 43)
Bosporus (bos′ pər əs) A strait connecting the Black Sea and the Sea of Marmara. (p. 42)
Boston (bôs′ tən) The capital of Massachusetts; 42°N, 71°W. (p. 15)
Botswana (bot swä′ nə) A country in south-central Africa. Capital, Gaborone. (p. 57)
Brahmaputra River (brä mə pü′ trə riv′ ər) A major river of southern Asia, flowing south from Tibet into the Bay of Bengal. Length, 1,770 miles (2,848 km). (p. 64)
Brasília (brə zēl′ yə) The capital of Brazil; 16°S, 48°W. (p. 35)
Brazil (brə zil′) The largest country in South America, on the Atlantic Ocean in the northeastern part of the continent. Capital, Brasília. (p. 35)
Brazzaville (bräz′ ə vēl) The capital of Congo; 4°S, 15°E. (p. 57)
Bridgetown (brij′ toun) The capital of Barbados; 14°N, 59°W. (p. 35)
British Isles (brit′ ish īlz) A group of islands off the western coast of Europe, made up of Britain, Ireland, and many smaller islands. (p. 42)
Brunei (brü nī′) A country on the northern coast of Borneo in southeastern Asia. Capital, Bandar Seri Begawan. (p. 65)
Brussels (brus′ əlz) The capital of Belgium; 51°N, 5°E. (p. 43)
Bucharest (bü′ kə rest) The capital and largest city of Romania; 44°N, 26°E. (p. 43)
Budapest (bü′ də pest) The capital and largest city of Hungary; 47°N, 19°E. (p. 43)
Buenos Aires (bwā′ nəs ī′ rəs) The capital of Argentina; 34°S, 58°W. (p. 35)
Bujumbura (bü jəm bůr′ ə) The capital of Burundi; 4°S, 31°E. (p. 57)
Bulgaria (bul gâr′ ē ə) A country in southeastern Europe. Capital, Sofia. (p. 43)
Burkina Faso (bər kē′ nə fä′ sō) A country in western Africa. Capital, Ouagadougou. (p. 57)
Burundi (bə run′ dē) A country in central Africa. Capital, Bujumbura. (p. 57)
Byelarus (bye lä rüs′) A country in eastern Europe, formerly part of the Soviet Union. Capital, Minsk. (p. 43)

C

Cairo (kī′ rō) The capital of Egypt; 30°N, 31°E. (p. 51)
California (kal ə fôr′ nyə) The most populated state of the United States, on the Pacific. Capital, Sacramento. (p. 15)
Cambodia (kam bō′ dē ə) A country in southeastern Asia, also known as Kampuchea. Capital, Phnom Penh. (p. 65)
Cameroon (kam ə rün′) A country in west-central Africa. Capital, Yaoundé. (p. 57)
Canada (kan′ ə də) A country in northern North America, bordering on the United States. Capital, Ottawa. (p. 15)
Canadian Shield (kə nā′ dē ən shēld) The plains and hills that surround Hudson Bay and cover about half of Canada. (p. 14)
Canary Islands (kə nâr′ ē ī′ ləndz) A Spanish island group in the northern Atlantic Ocean, off the northwestern coast of Africa. (p. 5)
Canberra (kan′ ber ə) The capital of Australia; 35°S, 149°E. (p. 71)
Cape Horn (kāp hôrn) A cape on an island of Tierra del Fuego, forming the southernmost tip of South America; 57°S, 64°W. (p. 34)

Cape of Good Hope (kāp əv gu̇d hōp) A cape at the southernmost tip of Africa, on the Atlantic Ocean; 34°S, 19°E. (p. 56)

Cape Town (kāp′ toun) The legislative capital of the Republic of South Africa; 34°S, 18°E. (p. 57)

Cape Verde (kāp vûrd) An island country in the northern Atlantic Ocean. Capital, Praia. (p. 4)

Caracas (kə rä′ kəs) The capital and largest city of Venezuela; 10°N, 66°W. (p. 35)

Caribbean Sea (kar ə bē′ ən sē) A sea bounded on the north and east by the West Indies, on the west by Central America, and on the south by South America. (p. 4)

Carpathian Mountains (kär pā′ thē ən moun′ tənz) A mountain system of eastern Europe extending southward toward the Black Sea. (p. 42)

Carson City (kär′ sən sit′ ē) The capital of Nevada; 39°N, 119°W. (p. 15)

Cascade Range (kas kād′ rānj) A mountain range in the western United States, extending from northern California through Oregon and into Washington. (p. 14)

Caspian Sea (kas′ pē ən sē) The largest inland body of water in the world, located in south-central Asia. (p. 42)

Castries (kas trēz′) The capital and largest city of St. Lucia; 14°N, 61°W. (p. 35)

Caucasus Mountains (kô′ kə səs moun′ tənz) A mountain range forming part of the boundary between Europe and Asia. (p. 42)

Cayenne (kī en′) The capital of French Guiana; 4°N, 52°W. (p. 35)

Celebes Sea (sel′ ə bēz sē) An arm of the Pacific Ocean, lying between the Philippines and Indonesia. (p. 64)

Central African Republic (sen′ trəl af′ ri kən ri pub′ lik) A country in central Africa. Capital, Bangui. (p. 57)

Central Valley (sen′ trəl val′ ē) A valley in central California. (p. 30)

Chad (chad) A country in north-central Africa. Capital, Ndjamena. (p. 57)

Chang River (chäng riv′ ər) The longest river in China. It is also known as the Chang Jiang and the Yangtze River. Length, 3,964 miles (6,342 km). (p. 64)

Charleston (chärlz′ tən) The capital of West Virginia; 38°N, 81°W. (p. 15)

Cherskiy Mountains (cher′ skē moun′ tənz) A mountain range in the northeastern part of Russia. (p. 42)

Chesapeake Bay (ches′ ə pēk bā) A bay of the Atlantic Ocean, partly surrounded by Virginia and Maryland. (p. 22)

Cheyenne (shī en′) The capital and largest city of Wyoming; 41°N, 104°W. (p. 15)

Chile (chil′ ē) A country on the southwestern coast of South America. Capital, Santiago. (p. 35)

China, People's Republic of (chī′ nə, pē′ pəlz ri pub′ lik əv) A country in eastern Asia. Capital, Beijing. (p. 65)

Coastal Plains (kōs′ təl plānz) The lowland plains of the United States lying along the Atlantic Ocean and the Gulf of Mexico. (p. 24)

Colombia (kə lum′ bē ə) A country in northwestern South America, on the Pacific Ocean and the Caribbean Sea. Capital, Bogotá. (p. 35)

Colombo (kə lum′ bō) The capital and chief port of Sri Lanka; 6°N, 79°E. (p. 65)

Colorado (kol ə rad′ ō) A state in the western United States. Capital, Denver. (p. 15)

Colorado River (kol ə rad′ ō riv′ ər) A river flowing from northern Colorado into the Gulf of California. Length, 1,450 miles (2,333 km). (p. 14)

Columbia (kə lum′ bē ə) The capital of South Carolina; 34°N, 81°W. (p. 15)

Columbus (kə lum′ bəs) The capital of Ohio; 40°N, 83°W. (p. 15)

Comoros (kom′ ə rōz) An island country off the southeastern coast of Africa. Capital, Moroni. (p. 57)

Conakry (kon′ ə krē) The capital of Guinea; 9°N, 13°W. (p. 57)

Concord (kon′ kôrd) The capital of New Hampshire; 43°N, 71°W. (p. 15)

Congo (kong′ go) A country in east-central Africa. Capital, Brazzaville. (p. 57)

Congo River (kong′ gō) The seventh-largest river in the world, located in central Africa. Length, 2,900 miles (4,640 km). (p. 11)

Connecticut (kə net′ i kət) A state in the northeastern United States. Capital, Hartford. (p. 15)

Connecticut River (kə net′ i kət riv′ ər) The longest river in New England, flowing from northern New Hampshire into Long Island Sound. Length, 407 miles (655 km). (p. 22)

Cook Islands (ku̇k ī′ ləndz) A group of islands east of Australia in the western part of the southern Pacific Ocean, a possession of New Zealand. (p. 71)

Copenhagen (kō′ pən hā gən) The capital and largest city of Denmark; 56°N, 12°E. (p. 43)

Coral Sea (kôr′ əl sē) A southwestern arm of the Pacific Ocean, off the coast of northeastern Australia. (p. 70)

Corsica (kôr′ si kə) A French island in the Mediterranean Sea, southeast of France. (p. 43)

Costa Rica (kos′ tə rē′ kə) A country in Central America, between Nicaragua and Panama. Capital, San José. (p. 35)

Côte d'Ivoire (kōt dē vwär′) A country in western Africa, formerly known as the Ivory Coast. Capital, Abidjan. (p. 57)

a cap; ā cake; ä father; är car; âr dare; ch chain; e hen; ē me; êr clear; hw where; i bib; ī kite; ng song; o top; ō rope; ô saw; oi coin; ôr fork; ou cow; sh show; th thin; th those; u sun; u̇ book; ü moon; ū cute; ûr term; ə about, taken, pencil, apron, helpful; ər letter, dollar, doctor

Crete (krēt) A Greek island in the Mediterranean Sea, southeast of mainland Greece. (p. 43)

Croatia (krō ā′ shə) A country in southeastern Europe, formerly part of Yugoslavia. Capital, Zagreb. (p. 43)

Cuba (kū′ bə) An island country in the Caribbean Sea, the largest and westernmost island of the West Indies. Capital, Havana. (p. 35)

Cyprus (sī′ prəs) An island country south of Turkey in the eastern Mediterranean Sea. Capital, Nicosia. (p. 51)

Czechoslovakia (chek ə slə vä′ kē ə) A country in central Europe. Capital, Prague. (p. 43)

D

Dakar (dä kär′) The capital and largest city of Senegal; 14°N, 17°W. (p. 57)

Damascus (də mas′ kəs) The capital and largest city of Syria; 33°N, 36°E. (p. 51)

Danube River (dan′ ūb riv′ ər) The second-longest river in Europe, flowing eastward from the southern part of Germany into the Black Sea. Length, 1,776 miles (2,858 km). (p. 42)

Dar es Salaam (där es sə läm′) The capital and largest city of Tanzania; 6°S, 39°E. (p. 57)

Darling River (dâr′ ling riv′ ər) A river in Australia, flowing southwest through western New South Wales to the Murray River. (p. 70)

Dead Sea (ded sē) A salt lake between Israel on the west and Jordan on the east. (p. 50)

Death Valley (deth val′ ē) A deep desert basin in southeastern California. It is the hottest and driest place in the United States and contains the lowest point in the Western Hemisphere. (p. 30)

Delaware (del′ ə wâr) A state in the eastern United States. Capital, Dover. (p. 15)

Delaware Bay (del′ ə wâr bā) An inlet of the Atlantic Ocean between Delaware and New Jersey. (p. 22)

Denmark (den′ märk) A country in northern Europe, between the North and Baltic seas. Capital, Copenhagen. (p. 43)

Denver (den′ vər) The capital of Colorado; 40°N, 103°W. (p. 15)

Des Moines (də moin′) The capital and largest city of Iowa; 41°N, 91°W. (p. 15)

Dhaka (dak′ ə) The capital and largest city of Bangladesh; 25°N, 91°E. (p. 65)

Djibouti (ji bü′ tē) A country in east Africa, on the Gulf of Aden. Capital, Djibouti. (p. 57)

Djibouti (ji bü′ tē) The capital of Djibouti; 11°N, 43°E. (p. 57)

Dnieper River (nē′ pər riv′ ər) A river flowing through eastern Europe into the Black Sea. Length, 1,368 miles (2,201 km). (p. 42)

Dniester River (nēs′ tər riv′ ər) A river flowing through Ukraine and Moldova into the Black Sea. Length, 840 miles (1,352 km). (p. 42)

Dodoma (dō′ də mə) A capital of Tanzania; 6°S, 35°E. (p. 57)

Doha (dō′ hä) The capital of Qatar; 25°N, 52°E. (p. 51)

Dominica (dom ə nē′ kə) A country in the eastern West Indies, one of the Windward Islands. Capital, Roseau. (p. 35)

Dominican Republic (də min′ i kən ri pub′ lik) A country in the central West Indies, occupying the eastern part of the island of Hispaniola. Capital, Santo Domingo. (p. 35)

Don River (don riv′ ər) A river flowing through Russia into the Sea of Azov. Length, 1,224 miles (1,969 km). (p. 42)

Dover (dō′ vər) The capital of Delaware; 39°N, 75°W. (p. 15)

Drakensberg Mountains (drä′ kənz bûrg moun′ tənz) A mountain range in southeastern Africa. (p. 56)

Dublin (dub′ lin) The capital and largest city of the Republic of Ireland; 53°N, 6°W. (p. 43)

Dushanbe (dyü shan′ bə) The capital of Tajikistan; 38°N, 69°E. (p. 43)

E

East China Sea (ēst chī′ nə sē) An arm of the Pacific Ocean between eastern China and the Ryukyu Islands. (p. 65)

Ecuador (ek′ wə dôr) A country on the northwestern coast of South America. Capital, Quito. (p. 35)

Edinburgh (ed′ ən bûr ō) The capital of Scotland; 55°N, 3°W. (p. 43)

Egypt (ē′ jipt) A country in northeastern Africa. Capital, Cairo. (p. 51)

El Aaiún (el ä ūn′) The capital of Western Sahara; 27°N, 13°W. (p. 51)

Elbe River (el′ bə riv′ ər) A river in central Europe, flowing from Czechoslovakia into the North Sea. Length, 720 miles (1,158 km). (p. 42)

Elburz Mountains (el bu̇rz′ moun′ tənz) A mountain range in northern Iran. (p. 50)

Ellesmere Island (elz′ mîr ī′ lənd) A large Canadian island in the Arctic Ocean, northwest of Greenland. (p. 15)

El Salvador (el sal′ və dôr) A country in western Central America. Capital, San Salvador. (p. 35)

English Channel (ing′ glish chan′ əl) A narrow body of water between Great Britain and northwestern Europe. (p. 42)

Equatorial Guinea (ē kwə tôr′ ē əl gin′ ē) A country in west-central Africa. Capital, Malabo. (p. 57)

Estonia (es tō′ nē ə) A country on the Baltic Sea, formerly part of the Soviet Union. Capital, Tallinn. (p. 43)

Ethiopia (ē thē ō′ pē ə) A country in eastern Africa. Capital, Addis Ababa. (p. 57)

Euphrates River (ū frā′ tēz riv′ ər) A river in the Middle East flowing from Turkey into the Persian Gulf. Length, 1,510 miles (2,430 km). (p. 50)

Europe (yu̇r′ əp) The world's sixth-largest continent. It lies between the Atlantic Ocean and Asia, from which it is separated by the Ural and Caucasus mountains. (p. 3)

F

Falkland Islands (fôk′ lənd ī′ ləndz) An island group in the southern Atlantic Ocean. A British dependency, they are also claimed by Argentina. (p. 34)

Federated States of Micronesia (fed′ ər ā ted stāts əv mī krō nē′ zhə) A group of Pacific islands administered by the United States. Capital, Kolonia. (p. 71)

Fiji (fē′ jē) A country consisting of some 800 islands north of New Zealand, in the southwestern Pacific Ocean. Capital, Suva. (p. 71)

Finland (fin′ lənd) A nation in northeastern Europe, on the Baltic Sea. Capital, Helsinki. (p. 43)

Florida (flôr′ i də) A state mostly on the southeastern peninsula of the United States. Capital, Tallahassee. (p. 15)

France (frans) A country in western Europe. Capital, Paris. (p. 43)

Frankfort (frangk′ fərt) The capital of Kentucky; 38°N, 84°W. (p. 15)

Freetown (frē′ toun) The capital of Sierra Leone; 8°N, 13°W. (p. 57)

French Guiana (french gē an′ ə) An overseas department of France, on the northeastern coast of South America. Capital, Cayenne. (p. 35)

French Polynesia (french pol ə nē′ zhə) A French possession in the southeastern Pacific Ocean consisting of several islands, including Tahiti. (p. 71)

Funafuti (fü nə fü′ tē) The capital of Tuvalu; 6°S, 166°E. (p. 71)

G

Gabon (ga bōn′) A country on the west coast of central Africa. Capital, Libreville. (p. 57)

Gaborone (gä bə rō′ nē) The capital of Botswana; 24°S, 25°E. (p. 57)

Gambia, (The) (gam′ bē ə) A country on the western coast of Africa. Capital, Banjul. (p. 57)

Gambia River (gam′ bē ə riv′ ər) A river in west Africa, flowing through Senegal and into the Atlantic Ocean. Length, 200 miles (322 km). (p. 56)

Ganges River (gan′ jēz riv′ ər) A river in northern India and Bangladesh, flowing from the Himalayas into the Bay of Bengal. Length, 1,560 miles (2,510 km). (p. 64)

Georgetown (jôrg′ toun) The capital and largest city of Guyana; 7°N, 58°W. (p. 35)

Georgia (jôr′ jə) A country in the Caucasus Mountain region, formerly part of the Soviet Union. Capital, Tbilisi. (p. 43)

Georgia (jôr′ jə) A state in the southeastern United States. Capital, Atlanta. (p. 15)

Germany (jûr′ mə nē) A country in north-central Europe. Capital, Berlin. (p. 43)

Ghana (gä′ nə) A country in western Africa, on the Gulf of Guinea. Capital, Accra. (p. 57)

Gibraltar (ji brôl′ tər) A British crown colony and seaport near the southern tip of Spain. (p. 43)

Gobi (gō′ bē) A large desert in southeastern Mongolia and northern China. (p. 64)

Gran Chaco (grän chä′ kō) A vast lowland region in south-central South America. (p. 34)

Grand Canyon (grand can′ yən) A large canyon in northwestern Arizona on the Colorado River; 36°N, 112°W. (p. 38)

Great Barrier Reef (grāt bar′ ē ər rēf) The largest barrier reef in the world, lying off the northeastern coast of Australia. (p. 70)

Great Basin (grāt bā′ sin) A low, bowl-shaped desert area located in the western part of the United States. (p. 30)

Great Britain (grāt brit′ ən) An island off the western coast of Europe that includes England, Scotland, and Wales. (p. 43)

Great Dividing Range (grāt di vīd′ ing rānj) Highlands extending along the eastern coast of Australia. (p. 70)

Greater Antilles (grāt′ ər an til′ ēz) An island group of the West Indies, including Cuba, Jamaica, Hispaniola, and Puerto Rico. (p. 34)

Great Lakes (grāt lāks) Five freshwater lakes lying along the border between Canada and the United States. They are Lake Superior, Lake Huron, Lake Michigan, Lake Erie, and Lake Ontario. (p. 14)

Great Plains (grāt plānz) The western, nearly treeless part of the Interior Plains of North America. (p. 14)

Great Salt Lake (grāt sôlt lāk) A lake in northwestern Utah, the largest salt lake in North America. (p. 14)

Great Slave Lake (grāt slāv lāk) A lake in the southwestern part of the Northwest Territories, Canada. (p. 14)

Greece (grēs) A country at the southern end of the Balkan Peninsula. Capital, Athens. (p. 43)

Greenland (grēn′ lənd) The largest island in the world, lying mostly within the Arctic Circle. (p. 14)

Grenada (gri nā′ də) An island country in the West Indies, one of the Windward Islands. Capital, St. George's. (p. 35)

Grenadines (gren′ ə dēnz) An island group in the Windward Islands, divided politically into Grenada and St. Vincent and the Grenadines. (p. 35)

Guadeloupe (gwä də lüp′) A French department in the West Indies, consisting of two islands in the Leeward Islands. (p. 35)

Guam (gwäm) An island in the western Pacific Ocean, east of the Philippines. It is a territory of the United States. Capital, Agana. (p. 5)

Guatemala (gwä tə mä′ lə) The northernmost country of Central America. Capital, Guatemala City. (p. 35)

Guatemala City (gwä tə mä′ lə sit′ ē) The capital and largest city of Guatemala; 14°N, 90°W. (p. 35)

Guinea (gin′ ē) A country on the Atlantic Ocean in western Africa. Capital, Conakry. (p. 57)

Guinea-Bissau (gin′ ē bē sou′) A country on the Atlantic Ocean in western Africa. Capital, Bissau. (p. 57)
Gulf of Aden (gulf əv ā′ dən) A western inlet of the Arabian Sea. (p. 50)
Gulf of Bothnia (gulf əv both′ nē ə) The northern arm of the Baltic Sea, between Sweden and Finland. (p. 43)
Gulf of California (gulf əv kal ə fôr′ nyə) A long inlet of the Pacific Ocean, just south of California. (p. 34)
Gulf of Mexico (gulf əv mek′ si kō) An arm of the Atlantic Ocean, between the United States and Mexico. (p. 34)
Gulf of Oman (gulf əv ō män′) A northern inlet of the Arabian Sea. (p. 50)
Gulf of St. Lawrence (gulf əv sānt lôr′ əns) An arm of the Atlantic Ocean, on the eastern coast of Canada, at the mouth of the St. Lawrence River. (p. 14)
Gulf of Tonkin (gulf əv ton′ kin′) An arm of the South China Sea, bordered by Vietnam and China. (p. 64)
Guyana (gī an′ ə) A country on the northeastern coast of South America. Capital, Georgetown. (p. 35)

H

Haiti (hā′ tē) A country in the Caribbean Sea, on the western part of the island of Hispaniola. Capital, Port-au-Prince. (p. 35)
Hanoi (ha noi′) The capital of Vietnam; 21°N, 105°E. (p. 65)
Harare (hə rär′ ā) The capital and largest city of Zimbabwe; 18°S, 13°E. (p. 57)
Harrisburg (har′ is bûrg) The capital of Pennsylvania; 40°N, 76°W. (p. 15)
Hartford (härt′ fərd) The capital of Connecticut; 41°N, 72°W. (p. 15)
Havana (hə van′ ə) The capital of Cuba; 23°N, 82°W. (p. 35)
Hawaii (hə wī′ ē) A state of the United States, made up of the Hawaiian Islands. It is the only island state of the United States and the only state not on the North American continent. Capital, Honolulu. (p. 15)
Helena (hel′ ə nə) The capital of Montana; 46°N, 112°W. (p. 15)
Helsinki (hel sing′ kē) The capital and largest city of Finland; 60°N, 24°E. (p. 43)
Himalayas (him ə lā′ əz) The highest mountain system in the world, forming part of the northern boundary of the Indian subcontinent. (p. 64)
Hindu Kush (hin′ dü küsh′) A mountain system of central Asia, largely in northeastern Afghanistan. (p. 64)
Hispaniola (his pən yō′ lə) An island in the Caribbean Sea, divided into the Dominican Republic and Haiti. (p. 34)
Honduras (hon dür′ əs) A country in northern Central America. Capital, Tegucigalpa. (p. 35)
Hong Kong (hong kong) A British crown colony off the southeastern coast of China. It will return to Chinese control after 1997; 22°N, 115°E. (p. 65)
Honiara (hō nē är′ ə) The capital of the Solomon Islands; 10°S, 146°E. (p. 71)
Honolulu (hon ə lü′ lü) The capital and largest city of Hawaii; 21°N, 157°W. (p. 15)
Huang River (hwäng riv′ ər) A large river that flows across China into the Yellow Sea. It is also known as the Huang Ho and the Yellow River. Length, 2,903 miles (4,644 km). (p. 64)
Hudson Bay (hud′ sən bā) A large inland sea in northeastern Canada. (p. 14)
Hudson River (hud′ sən riv′ ər) A river in eastern New York, flowing south into New York Bay. Length, 306 miles (492 km). (p. 22)
Hungary (hung′ gə rē) A country in east-central Europe. Capital, Budapest. (p. 43)

I

Iberian Peninsula (ī bîr′ ē ən pə nin′ sə lə) A large peninsula in southwestern Europe, between the Atlantic Ocean and the Mediterranean Sea. (p. 42)
Iceland (īs′ lənd) An island country in the northern Atlantic Ocean, between Greenland and Norway. Capital, Reykjavik. (p. 43)
Idaho (ī′ də hō) A state in the western United States. Capital, Boise. (p. 15)
Illinois (il ə noi′) A state in the north-central United States. Capital, Springfield. (p. 15)
India (in′ dē ə) A country in southern Asia. Capital, New Delhi. (p. 65)
Indiana (in dē an′ ə) A state in the north-central United States. Capital, Indianapolis. (p. 15)
Indianapolis (in dē ə nap′ ə lis) The capital and largest city of Indiana; 39°N, 86°W. (p. 15)
Indian Ocean (in′ dē ən ō′ shən) An ocean south of Asia, between Africa and Australia. (p. 3)
Indonesia (in də nē′ zhə) A country in southeastern Asia composed of thousands of islands. Capital, Jakarta. (p. 65)
Indus River (in′ dəs riv′ ər) A river flowing from Tibet through Kashmir and Pakistan into the Arabian Sea. Length, 1,800 miles (2,896 km). (p. 64)
Inner Mongolia (in′ ər môn gō′ lē ə) An autonomous region of China, in the northern part of the country. (p. 64)
Interior Plains (in tîr′ ē ər plānz) Plains covering much of the central part of North America. (p. 14)
Iowa (ī′ ə wə) A state in the north-central United States. Capital, Des Moines. (p. 15)
Iran (i ran′) A country in southwestern Asia. Capital, Tehran. (p. 51)
Iraq (i rak′) A country in southwestern Asia. Capital, Baghdad. (p. 51)
Ireland, Republic of (īr′ lənd, re pub′ lik əv) A country in northwestern Europe, on the island of Ireland. Capital, Dublin. (p. 43)
Irrawaddy River (ēr′ ə wod′ ē riv′ ər) A river flowing through Myanmar (Burma) into the Bay of Bengal. Length, 1,000 miles (1,600 km). (p. 64)
Irtysh River (îr tish′ riv′ ər) A river of central Asia, flowing northwest and north from the Altai Mountains in China into the Ob River in Siberia. Length, 2,747 miles (4,420 km). (p. 42)
Islamabad (is lä′ mə bäd) The capital of Pakistan; 33°N, 73°E. (p. 65)

Israel (iz′ rā əl) A country in southwestern Asia at the eastern end of the Mediterranean Sea. Capital, Jerusalem. (p. 51)
Isthmus of Panama (is′ məs əv pan′ ə mä) A narrow strip of land connecting North America and South America. (p. 34)
Italian Peninsula (i tal′ yən pə nin′ sə lə) A long peninsula in Southern Europe on which Italy is located. (p. 42)
Italy (it′ ə lē) A country in southern Europe, on the Mediterranean Sea. Capital, Rome. (p. 43)

J

Jackson (jak′ sən) The capital of Mississippi; 32°N, 90°W. (p. 15)
Jakarta (jə kär′ tə) The capital and largest city of Indonesia; 6°S, 107°E. (p. 65)
Jamaica (jə mā′ kə) An island country in the Caribbean Sea, south of Cuba. Capital, Kingston. (p. 35)
Japan (jə pan′) A country in the northern Pacific Ocean, off the eastern coast of Asia, consisting of a chain of islands. Capital, Tokyo. (p. 65)
Java Sea (jä′ və sē) An arm of the Pacific Ocean, in Indonesia. (p. 64)
Jefferson City (jef′ ər sən sit′ ē) The capital of Missouri; 38°N, 92°W. (p. 15)
Jerusalem (jə rü′ sə ləm) The capital of Israel; 31°N, 35°E. (p. 51)
Jordan (jôr′ dən) A country in southwestern Asia, east of and bordering Israel. Capital, Amman. (p. 51)
Juneau (jü′ nō) The capital of Alaska; 58°N, 136°W. (p. 15)

K

Kabul (kä bu̇l′) The capital of Afghanistan; 33°N, 69°E. (p. 65)
Kalahari Desert (kä lə här′ ē des′ ərt) A large desert in southern Africa. (p. 56)
Kampala (käm pä′ lə) The capital and largest city of Uganda; 1°N, 32°E. (p. 57)
Kansas (kan′ zəs) A state in the west-central United States. Capital, Topeka. (p. 15)
Karakoram Range (kär ə kôr′ əm rānj) A mountain system in central Asia, extending from northern Pakistan and India to southern China. (p. 64)
Kara Sea (kär′ ə sē) An arm of the Arctic Ocean, off the coast of north-central Russia. It is frozen most of the year. (p. 42)
Kathmandu (kat man dü′) The capital of Nepal; 27°N, 85°E. (p. 65)
Kazakhstan (kä zäk stän′) A country in central Asia, formerly part of the Soviet Union. Capital, Alma-Ata. (p. 43)
Kentucky (kən tuk′ ē) A state in the southeast region of the United States. Capital, Frankfort. (p. 15)
Kenya (ken′ yə) A country in eastern Africa. Capital, Nairobi. (p. 57)
Khartoum (kär tüm′) The capital of Sudan; 15°N, 32°E. (p. 57)
Kiev (kē əv′) The capital of Ukraine; 50°N, 30°E. (p. 43)
Kigali (ki gä′ lē) The capital of Rwanda; 1°S, 30°E. (p. 57)
Kingston (kingz′ tən) The capital and largest city of Jamaica; 18°N, 76°W. (p. 35)
Kingstown (kingz′ toun) The capital of St. Vincent and the Grenadines; 13°N, 61°W. (p. 35)
Kinshasa (kin shä′ sə) The capital and largest city of Zaire; 4°S, 15°E. (p. 57)
Kiribati (kîr i bä′ tē) An island nation in the central Pacific Ocean. Capital, Tarawa. (p. 71)
Kishinev (kish′ ə nev) The capital of Moldova; 46°N, 29°E. (p. 43)
Kolonia (kə lō′ nē ə) The capital of the Federated States of Micronesia; 3°N, 160°E. (p. 71)
Korea, North (kə rē ə, nôrth) A country occupying the northern part of the Korean Peninsula. Capital, Pyongyang. (p. 65)
Korea, South (kə rē ə, south) A country occupying the southern part of the Korean Peninsula. Capital, Seoul. (p. 65)
Kuala Lumpur (kwä′ lə lu̇m pu̇r′) The capital of Malaysia; 3°N, 101°E. (p. 65)
Kuril Islands (kyu̇r′ əl ī′ ləndz) A group of islands off the coast of Asia, northeast of Japan, east of and belonging to Russia. (p. 42)
Kuwait (kü wāt′) A country in the northeastern part of the peninsula of Arabia. Capital, Kuwait; 29°N, 47°E. (p. 51)
Kyrgyszstan (kêr′ giz stän) A country in central Asia, formerly part of the Soviet Union. Capital, Bishkek. (p. 43)

L

Lake Athabaska (lāk ath ə bas′ kə) A lake in Canada, on the northern Alberta-Saskatchewan border. (p. 14)
Lake Baikal (lāk bī käl′) A lake in southeast-central Russia. It is the deepest freshwater lake in the world. (p. 42)
Lake Chad (lāk chad) A lake in north-central Africa, at the southern edge of the Sahara. (p. 56)
Lake Champlain (lāk sham plān′) A lake on the border between New York and Vermont, extending into southwestern Quebec. (p. 22)
Lake Erie (lāk îr′ ē) The southernmost of the Great Lakes, on the U.S.-Canadian border. (p. 14)

a cap; ā cake; ä father; är car; âr dare; ch chain; e hen; ē me; êr clear; hw where; i bib; ī kite; ng song; o top; ō rope; ô saw; oi coin; ôr fork; ou cow; sh show; th thin; th those; u sun; u̇ book; ü moon; ū cute; ûr term; ə about, taken, pencil, apron, helpful; ər letter, dollar, doctor

Lake Eyre (lāk âr) A saltwater lake in Australia. (p. 70)
Lake Huron (lāk hyůr′ ən) The second largest of the Great Lakes, on the U.S.-Canadian border. (p. 14)
Lake Michigan (lāk mish′ i gən) The third-largest of the Great Lakes. It lies between Michigan and Wisconsin. (p. 14)
Lake Nasser (lāk näs′ ər) A lake in southern Egypt, formed in the 1960s as a result of the construction of the Aswan High Dam. (p. 50)
Lake of the Woods (lāk əv thə wůdz) A lake on the border of Minnesota and the Canadian provinces of Manitoba and Ontario. (p. 26)
Lake Ontario (lāk on târ′ ē ō) The smallest and easternmost of the Great Lakes, between New York and Canada. (p. 14)
Lake Superior (lāk sə pîr′ ē ər) The largest and northernmost of the Great Lakes, on the U.S.-Canadian border. (p. 14)
Lake Tanganyika (lāk tan gən yē′ kə) A lake in east-central Africa, lying between Zaire, Tanzania, and Zambia. (p. 56)
Lake Titicaca (lāk tit i kä′ kə) The largest lake in South America and the highest navigable lake in the world. (p. 34)
Lake Victoria (lāk vik tôr′ ē ə) The largest lake in Africa, located in the east-central part of the continent. (p. 57)
Lansing (lan′ sing) The capital of Michigan; 42°N, 84°W. (p. 15)
Laos (lä′ ōs) A country in southeastern Asia, between northern Thailand and northern Vietnam. Capital, Vientiane. (p. 65)
La Paz (lə päz′) The administrative capital of Bolivia; 16°S, 69°W. (p. 35)
Lapland (lap′ land) A region that includes northern Norway, northern Sweden, and northern Finland. (p. 42)
Laptev Sea (lap′ tef sē) An arm of the Arctic Ocean, off the northern coast of Russia. (p. 42)
Latvia (lat′ vē ə) A country on the Baltic Sea, formerly part of the Soviet Union. Capital, Riga. (p. 43)
Lebanon (leb′ ə non) A country in southwestern Asia, on the eastern shore of the Mediterranean Sea. Capital, Beirut. (p. 51)
Lena River (lē′ nə riv′ ər) A river in Russia, flowing through east-central Siberia into the Arctic Ocean. Length, 2,734 miles (4,374 km). (p. 42)
Lesotho (lə sō′ tō) A country in southern Africa, entirely surrounded by the Republic of South Africa. Capital, Maseru. (p. 57)
Lesser Antilles (les′ ər an til′ ēz) The islands, excluding the Bahamas, making up the eastern part of the West Indies, or Caribbean Islands. (p. 34)
Lhasa (lä′ sə) The capital of Tibet; 29°N, 91°E. (p. 65)
Liberia (lī bîr′ ē ə) A country on the west coast of Africa, first settled in 1822 by freed slaves from the United States. Capital, Monrovia. (p. 57)
Libreville (lē′ brə vil) The capital and largest city of Gabon; 1°N, 9°E. (p. 57)
Libya (lib′ ē ə) A country on the coast of northern Africa. Capital, Tripoli. (p. 51)
Liechtenstein (lik′ tən stīn) A country in central Europe, between Austria and Switzerland. Capital, Vaduz. (p. 43)
Lilongwe (li lông′ wā) The capital of Malawi; 13°S, 33°E. (p. 57)
Lima (lē′ mə) The capital of Peru; 12°S, 76°W. (p. 35)
Limpopo River (lim pō′ pō riv′ ər) A river in southeastern Africa, flowing from South Africa through Mozambique into the Indian Ocean. Length, 1,100 miles (1,774 km). (p. 56)
Lincoln (ling′ kən) The capital of Nebraska; 40°N, 96°W. (p. 15)
Lisbon (liz′ bən) The capital and largest city of Portugal; 38°N, 9°W. (p. 43)
Lithuania (lith ü ā′ nē ə) A country on the Baltic Sea, formerly part of the Soviet Union. Capital, Vilnius. (p. 43)
Little Rock (lit′ əl rok) The capital and largest city of Arkansas; 34°N, 92°W. (p. 15)
Ljubljana (lē ü blē än′ ə) The capital of Slovenia; 46°N, 14°E. (p. 43)
Loire River (lwär riv′ ər) The longest river in France, flowing from the south-central part of the country into the Bay of Biscay. Length, 625 miles (1,006 km). (p. 42)
Lomé (lō mā′) The capital of Togo; 6°N, 1°E. (p. 57)
London (lun′ dən) The capital and largest city of the United Kingdom; 51°N, 1°E. (p. 43)
Long Island Sound (lông ī′ lənd sound) An arm of the Atlantic Ocean, separating Connecticut from Long Island, New York. (p. 22)
Louisiana (lü ē zē an′ ə) A state in the southern United States, on the Gulf of Mexico and the Mississippi River. Capital, Baton Rouge. (p. 15)
Luanda (lü an′ də) The capital and largest city of Angola; 8°S, 14°E. (p. 57)
Lusaka (lü sä′ kə) The capital and largest city of Zambia; 15°S, 28°E. (p. 57)
Luxembourg (luk′ səm bûrg) A country in western Europe, bordering France, Belgium, and Germany. Capital, Luxembourg. (p. 43)
Luxembourg (luk′ səm bûrg) The capital and chief city of Luxembourg; 49°N, 6°E. (p. 43)

M

Macedonia (mas ə dō′ nē ə) A country in southeastern Europe, formerly part of Yugoslavia. Capital, Skopje. (p. 43)
Mackenzie River (mə ken′ zē riv′ ər) A river in northwestern Canada. Length, 2,635 miles (4,216 km). (p. 14)
Madagascar (mad ə gas′ kər) An island country in the Indian Ocean. Capital, Antananarivo. (p. 57)
Madison (mad′ ə sən) The capital of Wisconsin; 43°N, 89°W. (p. 15)
Madrid (mə drid′) The capital and largest city of Spain; 40°N, 4°W. (p. 43)
Maine (mān) A state in the northeastern United States. Capital, Augusta. (p. 15)
Majuro (mə jůr′ ō) The capital of the Marshall Islands; 8°N, 171°E. (p. 71)
Malabo (mə lä′ bō) The capital of Equatorial Guinea; 3°N, 8°E. (p. 57)
Malawi (mə lä′ wē) A country in southeastern Africa. Capital, Lilongwe. (p. 57)

Malaysia (mə lā′ zhə) A country in southeastern Asia, divided by the South China Sea. Capital, Kuala Lumpur. (p. 65)

Maldives (môl′ dēvz) A country of about 2,000 islands in the Indian Ocean, southwest of India. Capital, Malé. (p. 65)

Malé (mä′ lē) The capital of the Maldives; 5°N, 73°E. (p. 65)

Mali (mä′ lē) A country in western Africa. Capital, Bamako. (p. 57)

Malta (môl′ tə) A country consisting of an island group in the Mediterranean Sea. Capital, Valletta. (p. 43)

Managua (mə nä′ gwə) The capital and largest city of Nicaragua; 12°N, 86°W. (p. 35)

Manama (mə nam′ ə) The capital of Bahrain; 26°N, 50°E. (p. 51)

Manila (mə nil′ ə) The capital and largest city of the Philippines; 14°N, 121°E. (p. 65)

Maputo (mə pü′ tō) The capital of Mozambique; 26°S, 32°E. (p. 57)

Marshall Islands (mär′ shəl ī′ ləndz) An independent group of Pacific islands associated with the United States. Capital, Majuro. (p. 71)

Martinique (mär tə nēk′) A French island in the Caribbean Sea. (p. 35)

Maryland (mer′ ə lənd) A state in the eastern United States. Capital, Annapolis. (p. 15)

Maseru (maz′ ə rü) The capital of Lesotho; 29°S, 27°E. (p. 57)

Massachusetts (mas ə chü′ sits) A state in the northeastern United States. Capital, Boston. (p. 15)

Mauritania (môr i tā′ nē ə) A country on the northwestern coast of Africa. Capital, Nouakchott. (p. 57)

Mauritius (mô rish′ əs) An island country in the western Indian Ocean, east of Madagascar. Capital, Port Louis. (p. 5)

Mayotte (mä yot′) An island in the Indian Ocean. (p. 57)

Mbabane (bä bän′) The capital of Swaziland; 26°S, 31°E. (p. 57)

Mediterranean Sea (med i tə rā′ nē ən sē) A large, nearly landlocked arm of the Atlantic Ocean lying between Europe, Asia, and Africa. (p. 50)

Mekong River (mā′ kong′ riv′ ər) A river in Southeast Asia, flowing from western China southwest into the China Sea. Length, 2,600 miles (4,160 km). (p. 64)

Melanesia (mel ə nē′ zhə) One of the three main divisions of the Pacific islands. (p. 71)

Mesopotamia (mes ə pə tā′ mē ə) A historic region in southwestern Asia, between the Tigris and Euphrates rivers. (p. 50)

Mexico (mek′ si kō) A country in North America, south of and bordering the southwestern United States. Capital, Mexico City. (p. 35)

Mexico City (mek′ si kō sit′ ē) The capital and largest city of Mexico; 19°N, 99°W. (p. 35)

Michigan (mish′ i gən) A state in the north-central United States. Capital, Lansing. (p. 15)

Micronesia (mī krə nē′ zhə) One of the three main divisions of the Pacific islands. (p. 71)

Midway Islands (mid′ wā ī′ ləndz) A small island group in the north-central Pacific Ocean, administered by the United States. (p. 4)

Minnesota (min ə sō′ tə) A state in the north-central United States. Capital, St. Paul. (p. 15)

Minsk (minsk) The capital of Byelarus; 53°N, 27°E. (p. 43)

Mississippi (mis ə sip′ ē) A state in the southern United States. Capital, Jackson. (p. 15)

Mississippi River (mis ə sip′ ē riv′ ər) The Mississippi River, when combined with the Missouri River, forms the fourth-longest river system in the world. Length, 3,710 miles (5,936 km). (p. 14)

Missouri (mi zůr′ ē) A state in the central United States. Capital, Jefferson City. (p. 15)

Missouri River (mi zůr′ ē riv′ ər) A large river in the United States, flowing from Montana into the Mississippi River just north of St. Louis. (p. 14)

Mogadishu (mog ə dish′ ü) The capital of Somalia; 2°N, 45°E. (p. 57)

Moldova (mōl dō′ və) A country in eastern Europe, formerly part of the Soviet Union. Capital, Kishinev. (p. 43)

Monaco (mon′ ə kō) A country in southern Europe, on the Mediterranean Sea. Capital, Monaco; 43°N, 7°E. (p. 43)

Mongolia (mong gō′ lē ə) A country in central Asia, bordered by Russia and China. Capital, Ulaanbaatar. (p. 65)

Monrovia (mon rō′ vē ə) The capital and largest city of Liberia; 6°N, 10°W. (p. 57)

Montana (mon tan′ ə) A state in the northwestern United States. Capital, Helena. (p. 15)

Montevideo (mon tə vi dā′ ō) The capital of Uruguay; 34°S, 56°W. (p. 35)

Montgomery (mont gum′ ə rē) The capital of Alabama; 32°N, 86°W. (p. 15)

Montpelier (mont pēl′ yər) The capital of Vermont; 44°N, 72°W. (p. 15)

Morocco (mə rok′ ō) A country in northwestern Africa. Capital, Rabat. (p. 51)

Moscow (mos′ kou) The capital and largest city of Russia; 56°N, 38°W. (p. 43)

Mount Aconcagua (mount ak ən kä′ gwə) A mountain peak in the Andes Mountains, the highest in the Western Hemisphere. Height, 22,831 feet (6,959 m); 33°S, 70°W. (p. 34)

Mount Cook (mount kůk) The highest mountain in New Zealand. Height, 12,349 feet (3,764 m); 44°S, 170°E. (p. 70)

a cap; ā cake; ä father; är **car**; âr **dare**; ch **chain**; e **hen**; ē **me**; êr **clear**; hw **where**; i bib; ī **kite**; ng **song**; o **top**; ō **rope**; ô **saw**; oi **coin**; ôr **fork**; ou **cow**; sh **show**; th **thin**; th **those**; u **sun**; ů **book**; ü **moon**; ū **cute**; ûr **term**; ə **about**, tak**en**, penc**il**, apr**on**, help**ful**; ər lett**er**, doll**ar**, doct**or**

Mount Elbrus (mount el′ brüs) The highest peak of Europe. Height, 18,481 feet (5,633 m); 43°N, 43°E. (p. 42)

Mount Everest (mount ev′ ər əst) The highest mountain in the world, in the Himalayas. Height, 29,028 feet (8,848 m); 33°N, 87°E. (p. 64)

Mount Kilimanjaro (mount kil ə mən jär′ ō) The highest mountain in Africa, in northeastern Tanzania near the Kenyan border. Height, 19,340 feet (5,895 m); 3°S, 37°E. (p. 56)

Mount Kosciusko (mount kos ē us′ kō) The highest mountain in Australia. Height, 7,310 feet (2,228 m); 37°S, 148°E. (p. 70)

Mount McKinley (mount mə kin′ lē) The highest mountain in North America, in south-central Alaska. Height, 20,320 feet (6,194 m); 62°N, 150°W. (p. 14)

Mount St. Helens (mount sānt hel′ ənz) An active volcano in the state of Washington, in the Cascade Range. Height, 8,364 feet (2,549 m); 53°N, 122°W. (p. 30)

Mozambique (mō zəm bēk′) A country in southeastern Africa. Capital, Maputo. (p. 57)

Murray River (mûr′ ē riv′ ər) The Murray River, when combined with the Darling River, forms the longest river system in Australia. Length, 2,310 miles (3,718 km). (p. 70)

Muscat (mus′ kat) The capital of Oman; 23°N, 58°E. (p. 51)

Myanmar (mē′ ən mär) A country in southeastern Asia, formerly called Burma. Capital, Yangon. (p. 65)

N

Nairobi (nī rō′ bē) The capital of Kenya; 1°S, 36°E. (p. 57)

Namibia (nə mib′ ē ə) A country on the southwestern coast of Africa. Capital, Windhoek. (p. 57)

Nashville (nash′ vil) The capital of Tennessee; 36°N, 86°W. (p. 15)

Nassau (nas′ ô) The capital and largest city of the Bahamas; 25°N, 77°W. (p. 35)

Nauru (nä ü′ rü) An island country in the central Pacific Ocean, northeast of Australia. Capital, Yaren. (p. 71)

N'Djamena (ən jä′ mə nə) The capital of Chad; 3°N, 15°E. (p. 57)

Nebraska (nə bras′ kə) A state in the central United States. Capital, Lincoln. (p. 15)

Nepal (nə pôl′) A country in central Asia, bounded by India and Tibet. Capital, Kathmandu. (p. 65)

Netherlands (neth′ ər ləndz) A country in western Europe, on the North Sea. Capital, Amsterdam; Seat of government, The Hague. (p. 43)

Netherlands Antilles (neth′ ər ləndz an til′ ēz) A Dutch island group in the southern Caribbean Sea. (p. 35)

Nevada (nə vad′ ə) A state in the western United States. Capital, Carson City. (p. 15)

New Caledonia (nü kal i dō′ nē ə) A French island territory in the southern Pacific Ocean, east of Australia. (p. 70)

New Delhi (nü del′ ē) The capital of India; 28°N, 77°E. (p. 65)

New Guinea (nü gin′ ē) The second-largest island in the world, in the western Pacific Ocean, north of Australia. (p. 64)

New Hampshire (nü hamp′ shər) A state in the northeastern United States. Capital, Concord. (p. 15)

New Jersey (nü jûr′ zē) A state in the eastern United States. Capital, Trenton. (p. 15)

New Mexico (nü mek′ si kō) A state in the southwestern United States. Capital, Santa Fe. (p. 15)

New Siberian Islands (nü sī bîr′ ē ən ī′ ləndz) An island group in the Arctic Ocean off the northern tip of Russia. (p. 42)

New York (nü yôrk′) A state in the eastern United States. Capital, Albany. (p. 15)

New Zealand (nü zē′ lənd) An island country in the southern Pacific Ocean, east of Australia. Capital, Wellington. (p. 71)

Niagara Falls (nī ag′ rə fôlz) A waterfall on the Niagara River, between the United States and Canada. (p. 22)

Niamey (nyä mā′) The capital and largest city of Niger; 13°N, 2°E. (p. 57)

Nicaragua (nik ə rä′ gwə) The largest country of Central America. Capital, Managua. (p. 35)

Nicosia (nik ə sē′ ə) The capital of Cyprus; 35°N, 33°E. (p. 51)

Niger (nī′ jər) A country in western Africa. Capital, Niamey. (p. 57)

Nigeria (nī jîr′ ē ə) A country in western Africa, on the Gulf of Guinea. Capital, Abuja. (p. 57)

Niger River (nī′ jər riv′ ər) A river flowing from western Africa into the Gulf of Guinea. Length, 2,600 miles (4,183 km). (p. 56)

Nile River (nīl riv′ ər) The world's longest river, flowing from east-central Africa north into the Mediterranean Sea. Length, 4,100 miles (6,560 km). (p. 50)

Niue (nē ü′ ā) An island in the southern Pacific Ocean, a possession of New Zealand. (p. 71)

Norfolk Island (nôr fək′ ī′ lənd) An Australian island in the southern Pacific Ocean. (p. 70)

North America (nôrth ə mer′ ik ə) The world's third-largest continent, lying between the Pacific and Atlantic oceans. (p. 2)

North Carolina (nôrth kar ə lī′ nə) A state in the southeastern United States. Capital, Raleigh. (p. 15)

North China Plain (nôrth chī′ nə plān) A large, fertile plain lying north of the Qin Mountains in eastern China. (p. 64)

North Dakota (nôrth də kō′ tə) A state in the north-central United States. Capital, Bismarck. (p. 15)

Northern Mariana Islands (nôr′ thərn mâr ē an′ ə ī′ ləndz) A group of 16 islands in the western Pacific Ocean, administered by the United States. Capital, Saipan. (p. 71)

North Pole (nôrth pōl) The northernmost point on the earth; the northern end of the earth's axis, at 90°N. (p. 42)

North Sea (nôrth sē) A large arm of the Atlantic Ocean, between Great Britain and mainland Europe. (p. 42)

Norway (nôr′ wā) A country in northern Europe. Capital, Oslo. (p. 43)

Nouakchott (nwäk′ shot) The capital of Mauritania; 18°N, 15°W. (p. 57)

Nuku'alofa (nü kü ə lō′ fə) The capital and chief port of Tonga; 23°S, 175°W. (p. 71)

O

Ob River (ob riv′ ər) A river in western Siberia, in Russia, flowing northwest and north into the Arctic Ocean. Length, 3,362 miles (5,379 km). (p. 42)

Ohio (ō hī′ ō) A state in the north-central United States. Capital, Columbus. (p. 15)

Ohio River (ō hī′ ō riv′ ər) A river in the east-central United States, flowing from Pennsylvania southwest into the Mississippi River. Length, 981 miles (1,578 km). (p. 14)

Oklahoma (ō klə hō′ mə) A state in the south-central United States. Capital, Oklahoma City. (p. 15)

Oklahoma City (ō klə hō′ mə sit′ ē) The capital of Oklahoma; 35°N, 97°W. (p. 15)

Olympia (ō lim′ pē ə) The capital of Washington; 47°N, 122°W. (p. 15)

Oman (ō män′) A country in Asia, located on the southeastern coast of the Arabian Peninsula. Capital, Muscat. (p. 51)

Oregon (ôr′ i gon) A state in the northwestern United States, on the Pacific Ocean. Capital, Salem. (p. 15)

Orinoco River (ôr ə nō′ kō riv′ ər) A large river in South America, flowing through Venezuela into the Atlantic Ocean. Length, 1,600 miles (2,574 km). (p. 34)

Oslo (os′ lō) The capital and principal city of Norway; 59°N, 10°E. (p. 43)

Ottawa (ot′ ə wə) The capital of Canada; 46°N, 71°W. (p. 15)

Ouagadougou (wä gə dü′ gü) The capital of Burkina Faso; 6°N, 1°W. (p. 57)

Ozark Plateau (o′ zärk pla tō′) A low, hilly area in southern Missouri, northern Arkansas, and northeastern Oklahoma. (p. 24)

P

Pacific Ocean (pə sif′ ik ō′ shən) The world's largest body of water, lying between Asia and Australia on the west and North America and South America on the east. (p. 2)

Pago Pago (päng′ gō päng′ ō) The capital of American Samoa; 14°S, 172°W. (p. 71)

Pakistan (pak′ ə stan) A country in southern Asia. Capital, Islamabad. (p. 65)

Palau (pä lou′) A group of Pacific Ocean islands administered by the United States. Capital, Koror. (p. 5)

Pampas (pam′ pəz) The grass-covered plains of South America that cover much of central Argentina and parts of Uruguay. (p. 34)

Panama (pan′ ə mä) A country in Central America, on the Isthmus of Panama. Capital, Panama. (p. 35)

Panama City (pan′ ə mä sit′ ē) The capital of Panama; 8°N, 79°W. (p. 35)

Papua New Guinea (pap′ ū ə nü gin′ ē) An island nation in the southwestern Pacific Ocean. Capital, Port Moresby. (p. 71)

Paraguay (par′ ə gwā) A country in south-central South America. Capital, Asunción. (p. 35)

Paramaribo (par ə mar′ ə bō) The capital of Suriname; 5°N, 55°W. (p. 35)

Paraná River (par ə nä′ riv′ ər) A river in South America, flowing through Brazil, Paraguay, and Argentina into the Río de la Plata. Length, 2,485 miles (3,976 km). (p. 34)

Paris (par′ is) The capital and largest city of France; 49°N, 2°E. (p. 43)

Patagonia (pat ə gō′ nē ə) A region in southern Argentina. (p. 34)

Pennsylvania (pen səl vān′ yə) A state in the eastern United States. Capital, Harrisburg. (p. 15)

Persian Gulf (pûr′ zhən gulf) A body of water located between the Arabian Peninsula and Iran. (p. 50)

Peru (pə rü′) A country on the western coast of South America. Capital, Lima. (p. 35)

Philippines (fil′ ə pēnz) An island country in the western Pacific Ocean, southeast of China. Capital, Manila. (p. 65)

Phnom Penh (pə nom′ pen) The capital and largest city of Cambodia; 11°N, 104°E. (p. 65)

Phoenix (fē′ niks) The capital of Arizona; 33°N, 112°W. (p. 15)

Pierre (pîr) The capital of South Dakota; 44°N, 100°W. (p. 15)

Plateau of Iran (pla′ tō əv i ran′) A plateau in the northeastern part of Iran. (p. 50)

Plateau of Tibet (pla tō′ əv ti bet′) A high, dry plateau in southwestern China, north of the Himalayas. (p. 64)

Platte River (plat riv′ ər) A river flowing from central Nebraska into the Missouri River. Length, 310 miles (499 km). (p. 26)

Point Barrow (point bar′ ō) A small Alaskan peninsula, the northernmost point of the United States. (p. 14)

Poland (pō′ lənd) A country in central Europe on the Baltic Sea. Capital, Warsaw. (p. 43)

Polynesia (pol ə nē′ zhə) One of the three main divisions of the Pacific Ocean Islands. (p. 71)

Port-au-Prince (pôrt ō prins′) The capital of Haiti; 18°N, 17°W. (p. 35)

Port Louis (pôrt lü′ is) The capital and largest city of Mauritius; 20°S, 57°E. (p. 5)

Port Moresby (pôrt môrz′ bē) The capital of Papua New Guinea; 9°S, 147°E. (p. 71)

Port-of-Spain (pôrt′ əv spān′) The capital of Trinidad and Tobago; 10°N, 61°W. (p. 35)

Porto-Novo (pôr′ tō nō′ vō) The capital of Benin; 7°N, 3°E. (p. 57)

Portugal (pôr′ chə gəl) A country in southwestern Europe. Capital, Lisbon. (p. 43)

a cap; ā cake; ä father; är **car**; âr **dare**; ch **chain**; e **hen**; ē **me**; êr **clear**; hw **where**; i **bib**; ī **kite**; ng **song**; o **top**; ō **rope**; ô **saw**; oi **coin**; ôr **fork**; ou **cow**; sh **show**; th **thin**; th **those**; u **sun**; u̇ **book**; ü **moon**; ū **cute**; ûr **term**; ə **about**, tak**en**, penc**il**, apr**on**, help**ful**; ər lett**er**, doll**ar**, doct**or**

Port-Vila (pôrt′ vē′ lə) The capital of Vanuatu; 18°S, 174°E. (p. 71)
Potomac River (pə tō′ mək riv′ ər) A river in the eastern United States, flowing through West Virginia, Virginia, and Maryland into the Chesapeake Bay. Length, 285 miles (459 km). (p. 22)
Prague (präg) The capital and largest city of Czechoslovakia; 59°N, 14°E. (p. 43)
Praia (prī′ ə) The capital of Cape Verde; 15°N, 23°W. (p. 4)
Pretoria (pri tôr′ ē ə) The administrative capital of the Republic of South Africa; 25°S, 28°E. (p. 57)
Providence (prov′ i dəns) The capital and largest city of Rhode Island; 41°N, 71°W. (p. 15)
Puerto Rico (pwer′ tō rē′ kō) An island in the Greater Antilles of the West Indies. It is a commonwealth of the United States. Capital, San Juan. (p. 35)
Puget Sound (pū′ jit sound) An inlet of the Pacific Ocean, extending into the state of Washington. (p. 30)
Pyongyang (pyung′ yäng′) The capital of North Korea; 39°N, 125°E. (p. 65)
Pyrenees (pir′ ə nēz) A mountain range in the southwestern part of western Europe, extending from the Bay of Biscay to the Mediterranean Sea. (p. 42)

Q

Qatar (kä′ tər) A country in southwestern Asia, on the Arabian Peninsula. Capital, Doha. (p. 51)
Quito (kē′ tō) The capital of Ecuador; 1°S, 78°W. (p. 35)

R

Rabat (rə bät′) The capital of Morocco; 33°N, 6°W. (p. 51)
Raleigh (rô′ lē) The capital of North Carolina; 35°N, 78°W. (p. 15)
Red River (red riv′ ər) A river flowing from southwestern Oklahoma into the Mississippi River. Length, 1,270 miles (2,043 km). (p. 28)
Red Sea (red sē) A narrow sea located between the Arabian Peninsula and northeastern Africa. (p. 50)
Réunion (rē ūn′ yən) A French island off the coast of Madagascar in the Indian Ocean. (p. 57)
Reykjavik (rā′ kyə vēk) The capital and largest city of Iceland; 64°N, 21°W. (p. 43)
Rhine River (rīn riv′ ər) A river in Western Europe that flows from eastern Switzerland into the North Sea. Length, 700 miles (1,126 km). (p. 42)
Rhode Island (rōd ī′ lənd) A state in the northeastern United States. Capital, Providence. (p. 15)
Richmond (rich′ mənd) The capital of Virginia; 37°N, 77°W. (p. 15)
Riga (rē′ gə) The capital of Latvia; 56°N, 25°E. (p. 43)
Río de la Plata (rē′ ō dā lä plät′ ə) An estuary of the Paraná and Uruguay rivers, in South America. (p. 34)
Rio Grande (rē′ ō grand) A river flowing from southwestern Colorado into the Gulf of Mexico and forming the border between the United States and Mexico. Length, 1,885 miles (3,033 km). (p. 14)
Riyadh (rē yäd′) The capital of Saudi Arabia; 25°N, 47°E. (p. 51)
Rocky Mountains (rok′ ē moun′ tənz) The high, rugged mountains that stretch along the western part of North America from Alaska south to New Mexico. (p. 14)
Romania (rō mā′ nē ə) A country in southeastern Europe. Capital, Bucharest. (p. 43)
Rome (rōm) The capital of Italy; 42°N, 13°E. (p. 43)
Roseau (rō zō′) The capital of Dominica; 15°N, 61°W. (p. 35)
Rub' al-Khali (rùb al käl′ ē) A desert region in the Arabian Peninsula. Also, Great Sandy Desert. (p. 50)
Rwanda (rü än′ də) A country in east-central Africa. Capital, Kigali. (p. 57)
Russia (rush′ ə) A country in eastern Europe and northern Asia, formerly part of the Soviet Union. Capital, Moscow. (p. 43)

S

Sacramento (sak rə men′ tō) The capital of California; 39°N, 121°W. (p. 15)
Sahara (sə har′ ə) A desert in north-central Africa, the largest in the world. (p. 50)
Salem (sā′ ləm) The capital of Oregon; 44°N, 123°W. (p. 15)
Salt Lake City (sôlt lāk sit′ ē) The capital and largest city of Utah; 40°N, 111°W. (p. 15)
San'a (sä nä′) The capital of Yemen; 15°N, 44°E. (p. 51)
San Francisco Bay (san frən sis′ kō bā) An inlet of the Pacific Ocean, on the central coast of California. (p. 30)
San José (san hō zā′) The capital and largest city of Costa Rica; 9°N, 84°W. (p. 35)
San Juan (san hwän′) The capital of Puerto Rico; 18°N, 66°W. (p. 35)
San Marino (san mə rē′ nō) A small country in Europe completely surrounded by Italy. Capital, San Marino. (p. 43)
San Marino (san mə rē′ nō) The capital of San Marino; 44°N, 12°E. (p. 43)
San Salvador (san sal′ və dôr) The capital and largest city of El Salvador; 13°N, 85°W. (p. 35)
Santa Fe (san′ tə fā′) The capital of New Mexico; 35°N, 106°W. (p. 15)
Santiago (san tē ä′ gō) The capital and largest city of Chile; 34°S, 71°W. (p. 35)
Santo Domingo (san′ tō də ming′ gō) The capital and largest city of the Dominican Republic; 18°N, 69°W. (p. 35)
São Francisco River (soun frän sēs′ kù riv′ ər) A river in South America, flowing into the Atlantic Ocean. Length, 1,800 miles (2,896 km). (p. 34)
São Tomé (soun tù mā′) The capital of São Tomé and Príncipe; 0°, 7°E. (p. 57)
São Tomé and Príncipe (soun tù mā′ ənd prēn′ si pā) An island country located off the west coast of Africa, in the Gulf of Guinea. Capital, São Tomé. (p. 57)
Sarajevo (sär ə yā′ vō) The capital of Bosnia and Herzegovina; 44°N, 18°E. (p. 43)
Sardinia (sär din′ ē ə) An Italian island in the Mediterranean Sea, west of Italy. (p. 43)
Saudi Arabia (sä ü′ dē ə rā′ bē ə) A country in southwestern Asia, occupying most of the Arabian Peninsula. Capital, Riyadh. (p. 51)

Scandinavian Peninsula (skan də nā′ vē ən pə nin′ sə lə) A large peninsula in northern Europe, divided between Norway and Sweden. (p. 42)

Sea of Okhotsk (sē əv ō kotsk′) An arm of the Pacific Ocean, on the east coast of Russia. (p. 42)

Seine River (sān riv′ ər) A river flowing from eastern France northward into the English Channel. Length, 485 miles (780 km). (p. 42)

Senegal (sen i gôl′) A country in western Africa, on the Atlantic. Capital, Dakar. (p. 57)

Senegal River (sen i gôl′ riv′ ər) A river in western Africa, on the southern border of the Sahara, flowing into the Atlantic. Length, 1,000 miles (1,609 km). (p. 56)

Seoul (sōl) The capital and largest city of South Korea; 37°N, 127°E. (p. 65)

Seychelles (sā shel′) An island country in the western Indian Ocean, northeast of Madagascar. Capital, Victoria. (p. 57)

Siberia (sī bîr′ ē ə) A region of Russia, extending from the Ural Mountains to the Pacific. (p. 43)

Sicily (sis′ ə lē) An Italian island in the Mediterranean Sea, off the southwestern tip of Italy. (p. 43)

Sierra Leone (sē er′ ə lē ō′ nē) A country on the western coast of Africa. Capital, Freetown. (p. 57)

Sierra Madre (sē er′ ə mä′ drā) A mountain system in eastern and western Mexico. (p. 34)

Sierra Nevada (sē er′ ə nə vad′ ə) A mountain range in eastern California. (p. 14)

Sinai (sī′ nī) A triangular desert area in northeastern Egypt. (p. 50)

Singapore (sing′ ə pôr) A country off the southern tip of the Malay Peninsula. Capital, Singapore; 1°N, 103°E. (p. 65)

Skopje (skôp′ yā) The capital of Macedonia; 42°N, 22°W. (p. 43)

Slovenia (slō vēn′ ē ə) A country in southeastern Europe, formerly part of Yugoslavia. Capital, Ljubljana. (p. 43)

Snake River (snāk riv′ ər) A river in the northwestern United States, the principal tributary of the Columbia River. Length, 1,038 miles (1,670 km). (p. 30)

Sofia (sō′ fē ə) The capital of Bulgaria; 43°N, 23°E. (p. 43)

Solomon Islands (sol′ ə mən ī′ ləndz) An island country in the southwestern Pacific Ocean. Capital, Honiara. (p. 71)

Somalia (sō mäl′ yə) A country in eastern Africa, on the Indian Ocean and Gulf of Aden. Capital, Mogadishu. (p. 57)

South Africa, Republic of (south af′ ri kə, ri pub′ lik əv) A country in southern Africa. Administrative capital, Pretoria; judicial capital, Bloemfontein; legislative capital, Cape Town. (p. 57)

South America (south ə mer′ ik ə) The fourth-largest continent in the world, in the Western Hemisphere. (p. 2)

South Carolina (south kar ə lī′ nə) A state in the southeastern United States. Capital, Columbia. (p. 15)

South China Sea (south chī′ nə sē) A part of the Pacific Ocean, bounded by southeastern China, Vietnam, the Malay Peninsula, Borneo, and the Philippines. (p. 64)

South Dakota (south də kō′ tə) A state in the north-central United States. Capital, Pierre. (p. 15)

South Pole (south pōl) The southernmost point of the earth; 90°S. (p. 71)

South Sandwich Islands (south sand′ wich ī′ ləndz) A group of islands in the Atlantic Ocean near Antarctica. (p. 71)

Spain (spān) A country in southwestern Europe, on the Iberian Peninsula. Capital, Madrid. (p. 43)

Springfield (spring′ fēld) The capital of Illinois; 39°N, 89°W. (p. 15)

Sri Lanka (srē läng′ kə) An island country in the Indian Ocean, east of the southern tip of India. Capital, Colombo. (p. 65)

St. George's (sānt jôr′ jiz) The capital and largest city of Grenada; 12°N, 61°W. (p. 35)

St. John's (sānt jonz) The capital of Antigua and Barbuda; 17°N, 61°W. (p. 35)

St. Kitts and Nevis (sānt kits′ nē′ vis) A West Indian island nation made up of two of the Leeward Islands, St. Kitts (also called St. Christopher) and Nevis. Capital, Basseterre. (p. 35)

St. Lawrence River (sānt lôr′ əns riv′ ər) A river in North America flowing from Lake Ontario northeast into the Gulf of St. Lawrence. Length, 800 miles (1,287 km). (p. 14)

St. Lucia (sānt lü′ shə) A West Indian island nation, one of the Windward Islands. Capital, Castries. (p. 35)

St. Paul (sānt pôl′) The capital of Minnesota; 44°N, 93°W. (p. 15)

Strait of Magellan (strāt əv mə jel′ ən) A strait at the southern tip of mainland South America, linking the Atlantic and the Pacific oceans. (p. 34)

St. Vincent and the Grenadines (sānt′ vin′ sənt and t͟hə gren′ ə dēnz) A West Indian island nation in the Windward Islands. Capital, Kingstown. (p. 35)

Stockholm (stok′ hōm) The capital and largest city of Sweden; 59°N, 18°E. (p. 43)

Sucre (sü′ krā) The judicial capital of Bolivia; 18°S, 65°W. (p. 35)

Sudan (sü dan′) A country in northeastern Africa. Capital, Khartoum. (p. 57)

Suez Canal (sü ez′ kə nal′) A canal in northeastern Egypt, connecting the Mediterranean and Red seas. (p. 50)

a c**a**p; ā c**a**ke; ä f**a**ther; är c**ar**; âr d**are**; ch **ch**ain; e h**e**n; ē m**e**; êr cl**ear**; hw **wh**ere; i b**i**b; ī k**i**te; ng so**ng**; o t**o**p; ō r**o**pe; ô s**aw**; oi c**oi**n; ôr f**or**k; ou c**ow**; sh **sh**ow; th **th**in; t͟h **th**ose; u s**u**n; u̇ b**oo**k; ü m**oo**n; ū c**u**te; ûr t**er**m; ə **a**bout, tak**e**n, penc**i**l, apr**o**n, helpf**u**l; ər lett**er**, doll**ar**, doct**or**

Suriname (sůr′ ə näm) A country on the northeastern coast of South America. Capital, Paramaribo. (p. 35)
Susquehanna River (sus kwə han′ ə riv′ ər) A river flowing through New York, Pennsylvania, and Maryland. Length, 444 miles (710 km). (p. 22)
Suva (sü′ və) The capital of Fiji; 17°S, 168°E. (p. 71)
Swaziland (swä′ ze land) A country in southeastern Africa. Capital, Mbabane. (p. 57)
Sweden (swē′ dən) A country in northern Europe. Capital, Stockholm. (p. 43)
Switzerland (swit′ sər lənd) A mountainous country in central Europe. Capital, Bern. (p. 43)
Syria (sîr′ ē ə) A country in southwestern Asia. Capital, Damascus. (p. 51)

T

Taipei (tī′ pā′) The capital of Taiwan; 25°N, 121°E. (p. 65)
Taiwan (tī′ wän′) An island country in the western Pacific Ocean. Capital, Taipei. (p. 65)
Tajikistan (tä jik′ i stän) A country in central Asia, formerly part of the Soviet Union. Capital, Dushanbe. (p. 43)
Tallahassee (tal ə has′ ē) The capital of Florida; 30°N, 84°W. (p. 15)
Tallinn (tal′ ən) The capital of Estonia; 59°N, 25°E. (p. 43)
Tanzania (tan zə nē′ ə) A country in east-central Africa. Capitals, Dodoma and Dar es Salaam. (p. 57)
Tarawa (tə rä′ wə) The capital of Kiribati; 1°N, 174°E. (p. 71)
Tashkent (tash kent′) The capital of Uzbekistan; 41°N, 69°E. (p. 43)
Tbilisi (tə bil′ ə sē) The capital of Georgia; 42°N, 45°E. (p. 43)
Tegucigalpa (tə gü si gal′ pə) The capital of Honduras; 14°N, 87°W. (p. 35)
Tehran (te rän′) The capital and largest city of Iran; 35°N, 51°E. (p. 51)
Tennessee (ten ə sē′) A state in the southeastern United States. Capital, Nashville. (p. 15)
Texas (tek′ səs) A state in the south-central United States. Capital, Austin. (p. 15)
Thailand (tī′ land) A country in southeastern Asia. Capital, Bangkok. (p. 65)
Thimphu (tim′ pü) The capital of Bhutan; 28°N, 90°E. (p. 65)
Tibet (ti bet′) A country in southwestern China, claimed by the People's Republic of China. Capital, Lhasa. (p. 65)
Tierra del Fuego (tyer ə del fwā′ gō) An archipelago at the southern tip of South America. (p. 34)
Tigris River (tī′ gris riv′ ər) A river in southwestern Asia, flowing from eastern Turkey into the Persian Gulf. Length, 1,180 miles (1,899 km). (p. 50)
Timor Sea (tē′ môr sē) An arm of the Indian Ocean, between Indonesia and Australia. (p. 64)
Tiranë (ti rä′ nə) The capital and largest city of Albania; 41°N, 20°E. (p. 43)
Togo (tō′ gō) A country in western Africa on the Gulf of Guinea. Capital, Lomé. (p. 57)
Tokelau (tō′ kə lou) A group of three atolls administered by New Zealand, in the Pacific Ocean. (p. 71)
Tokyo (tō′ kyō) The capital and largest city of Japan; 36°N, 140°E. (p. 65)
Tonga (tong′ gə) A country consisting of islands in the southern Pacific Ocean. Capital, Nuku'alofa. (p. 71)
Topeka (tə pē′ kə) The capital of Kansas; 39°N, 35°W. (p. 15)
Trenton (tren′ tən) The capital of New Jersey; 40°N, 70°W. (p. 15)
Trinidad and Tobago (trin′ i dad ənd tə bā′ gō) A country consisting of the West Indian islands of Trinidad and Tobago. Capital, Port-of-Spain. (p. 35)
Tripoli (trip′ ə lē) The capital and largest city of Libya; 32°N, 13°E. (p. 51)
Tunis (tü′nis) The capital and largest city of Tunisia; 37°N, 10°E. (p. 51)
Tunisia (tü nē′ zhə) A country on the northern coast of Africa, on the Mediterranean Sea. Capital, Tunis. (p. 51)
Turkey (tûr′ kē) A country in western Asia and southeastern Europe. Capital, Ankara. (p. 51)
Turkmenistan (tûrk men′ i stän) A country in central Asia, formerly part of the Soviet Union. Capital, Ashkhabad. (p. 43)
Tuvalu (tü vä′ lü) An island country in the central Pacific Ocean. Capital, Funafuti. (p. 71)

U

Uganda (ū gan′ də) A country in east-central Africa. Capital, Kampala. (p. 57)
Ukraine (ū krān′) A country in eastern Europe, formerly part of the Soviet Union. Capital, Kiev. (p. 43)
Ulaanbaatar (ü′ län bä′ tôr) The capital and largest city of Mongolia; 47°N, 107°E. (p. 65)
United Arab Emirates (ū nī′ tid ar′ əb em′ ər its) A country composed of seven sheikdoms on the east-central coast of the Arabian Peninsula. Capital, Abu Dhabi. (p. 51)
United Kingdom (ū nī′ tid king′ dəm) A country in Europe, composed of England, Scotland, Wales, and Northern Ireland. Capital, London. (p. 43)
United States (ū nī′ tid stāts) A country mainly in North America, consisting of 50 states. Capital, Washington, D.C. (p. 15)
Ural Mountains (yůr′ əl moun′ tənz) A mountain system extending north to south in the east-central Soviet Union, forming part of the traditional boundary between Europe and Asia. (p. 42)
Uruguay (yůr′ ə gwā) A country on the southeastern coast of South America. Capital, Montevideo. (p. 35)
Uruguay River (yůr′ ə gwā riv′ ər) A river in southeastern South America, flowing into the Río de la Plata. Length, 1,000 miles (1,609 km). (p. 34)
Utah (u′ tô) A state in the western United States. Capital, Salt Lake City. (p. 15)
Uzbekistan (uz bek′ i stän) A country in central Asia, formerly part of the Soviet Union. Capital, Tashkent. (p. 43)

V

Vaduz (vä düts′) The capital of Liechtenstein; 47°N, 9°E. (p. 43)

Valletta (və let′ ə) The capital of Malta; 35°N, 14°E. (p. 43)

Vanuatu (van ü ä′ tü) A country in the southwestern Pacific Ocean. Capital, Port-Vila. (p. 71)

Vatican City (vat′ i kən sit′ ē) An independent state located within Rome. Seat of the Roman Catholic Church; 42°N, 12°E. (p. 43)

Venezuela (ven ə zwā′ lə) A country in South America, on the Caribbean Sea. Capital, Caracas. (p. 35)

Verkhoyansk Mountains (vyer kə yansk′ moun′ tənz) A mountain range in the northeastern part of Russia, south of the Arctic Ocean. (p. 42)

Vermont (vər mont′) A state in the northeastern United States. Capital, Montpelier. (p. 15)

Victoria (vik tôr′ ē ə) The capital of Seychelles; 6°S, 54°E. (p. 57)

Vienna (vē en′ ə) The capital and largest city of Austria; 48°N, 16°E. (p. 43)

Vientiane (vyen tyän′) The capital and largest city of Laos; 18°N, 103°E. (p. 65)

Vietnam (vē et näm′) A country in southeastern Asia. Capital, Hanoi. (p. 65)

Vilnius (vil′ nē əs) The capital of Lithuania; 55°N, 25°E. (p. 43)

Vinson Massif (vint′ sən ma sēf′) The sixth-highest mountain in the world, located in Antarctica. Height, 16,864 feet (5,140 m). (p. 71)

Virginia (vər jin′ yə) A state in the eastern United States. Capital, Richmond. (p. 15)

Virgin Islands (vûr′ jin ī′ ləndz) An island group of the Caribbean. It is divided politically between the United States and Great Britain. (p. 35)

Volga River (vol′ gə riv′ ər) A river in western Russia. Length, 2,194 miles (3,530 km). (p. 42)

W

Wake Island (wāk ī′ lənd) An atoll in the Pacific Ocean, administered by the United States. (p. 5)

Warsaw (wôr′ sô) The capital and largest city of Poland; 52°N, 21°E. (p. 43)

Washington (wô′ shing tən) A state in the northwestern United States. Capital, Olympia. (p. 15)

Washington, D.C. (wô′ shing tən dē sē) The capital of the United States. It is also known as the District of Columbia; 38°N, 77°W. (p. 15)

Wellington (wel′ ing tən) The capital of New Zealand; 41°S, 174°E. (p. 71)

Western Sahara (wes′ tûrn sə har′ ə) A territory on the northwestern coast of Africa, claimed by Morocco. Capital, El Aaiún. (p. 51)

Western Samoa (wes′ tûrn sə mō′ ə) An island country in the southern Pacific Ocean, east of Australia, consisting of the western islands of Samoa. Capital, Apia. (p. 71)

West Virginia (west vər jin′ yə) A state in the eastern United States. Capital, Charleston. (p. 15)

Windhoek (vint′ hu̇k) The capital of Namibia; 22°S, 17°E. (p. 57)

Wisconsin (wis kon′ sin) A state in the north-central United States. Capital, Madison. (p. 15)

Wrangel Island (rang′ gəl ī′ lənd) An island off the coast of Russia, in the Arctic Ocean. (p. 42)

Wyoming (wī ō′ ming) A state in the western United States. Capital, Cheyenne. (p. 15)

Y

Yangon (yan′ gôn′) The capital of Myanmar (Burma), formerly called Rangoon; 16°N, 96°E. (p. 65)

Yaoundé (yä ün dā′) The capital of Cameroon; 4°N, 11°E. (p. 57)

Yaren (yâr′ ən) The capital of Nauru; 0°, 168°E. (p. 71)

Yellow Sea (yel′ ō sē) A shallow arm of the Pacific Ocean, between northeastern China and North Korea and South Korea. (p. 64)

Yemen (yem′ ən) A country in the southwestern part of the Arabian Peninsula, on the Red Sea. Capital, San'a. (p. 51)

Yerevan (yer ə vän′) The capital of Armenia; 40°N, 45°E. (p. 43)

Yucatán (ū kə tan′) A peninsula between the Gulf of Mexico and the Caribbean Sea. (p. 34)

Yugoslavia (ū gō slä′ vē ə) A country in southeastern Europe. Capital, Belgrade. (p. 43)

Z

Zagreb (zäg′ reb) The capital of Croatia; 45°N, 16°W. (p. 43)

Zagros Mountains (zag′ rəs moun′ tənz) A mountain range extending along the borders of Iran and Iraq. (p. 50)

Zaire (zä îr′) A country in central Africa. Capital, Kinshasa. (p. 57)

Zambia (zam′ bē ə) A country in south-central Africa. Capital, Lusaka. (p. 57)

Zanzibar (zan′ zə bär) An island in the Indian Ocean, off the eastern coast of Africa, part of Tanzania. (p. 56)

Zimbabwe (zim bäb′ wē) A country in south-central Africa. Capital, Harare. (p. 57)

a cap; ā cake; ä father; är car; âr dare; ch chain; e hen; ē me; êr clear; hw where; i bib; ī kite; ng song; o top; ō rope; ô saw; oi coin; ôr fork; ou cow; sh show; th thin; th̲ those; u sun; u̇ book; ü moon; ū cute; ûr term; ə about, taken, pencil, apron, helpful; ər letter, dollar, doctor

PHOTOGRAPHY CREDITS

vi: t.l. Mike Yamashita/Woodfin Camp; t.r. Guido Alberto Rossi/ The Image Bank; m.l. Jeff Kida/Adstock Photos; m. David Falconer; m.r. Terry Madison/The Image Bank. vi–1 b.: NASA. 1: b. Matt Bradley; t.m. Morton Beebe/The Image Bank; t.r. Adam Woolfitt/Woodfin Camp; m.l. Steve Satushek/The Image Bank; m.r. Tom Hollyman/Photo Researchers, Inc.

12: r. Berenholtz/The Stock Market; t.l. Michal Heron; t.r. Richard Haynes Jr.; m.l. Rick Furniss/Alaska Photo; m. Michal Heron; m.r. David Falconer; b.l. Grant Heilman Photography Inc.; b.m. Paolo Koch/Photo Researchers, Inc. 13: t.r. Chris Sorenson/The Stock Market; b.l. Brett Froomer/The Image Bank; b.r. Steve Murray/ After Image, Inc.

32: t.l. Robert Frerck/Odyssey Productions; t.m. Robert Frerck/ Odyssey Productions; t.r. M. Isy Schwart/The Image Bank; m. Luis Villota/The Stock Market; b.l. Steve Elmore/The Stock Market; b.r. Photos Michael Holford. 32–33: b. Dan Helms/ Duomo. 33: t.m. Paul Crum/Photo Researchers, Inc.; t.r. James H. Carmichael, Jr./The Image Bank; m.r. Peter Frey/The Image Bank; b.m. Luis Villota/The Stock Market.

40: t.l. John Launois/Black Star; t.m. Jim Richardson/Woodfin Camp; t.r. Tass/SOVFOTO/Eastfoto; m.l. R. Steedman/The Stock Market; m. Dana Hyde/Photo Researchers, Inc.; b.m. J. Messer-schmidt/The Stock Market. 40–41: b. Giansanti/Sygma. 41: b.m. Luis Villota/The Stock Market; b.r. Serguei Fedorov/Woodfin Camp.

48: t.l. Guido Alberto Rossi/The Image Bank; t.r. Robert Frerck/ Odyssey Productions; m.l. Geoff Juckes/The Stock Market; m.r. Mort Pechter/The Stock Market; b.m. Charles Henneghien/Bruce Coleman. 48–49 b. George Holton/Photo Researchers, Inc. 49: t.r. Robert Frerck/Woodfin Camp; m.r. Kay Chernush/The Image Bank; b.r. Gerhardt Liebmann/Photo Researchers, Inc.

54: t.l. M. & E. Bernheim/Woodfin Camp; t.r. Pedrocoll/The Stock Market; m. Alon Reininger/Woodfin Camp; b.l. Peter Turnley/Black Star. 54–55 b. Breck P. Kent. 55: t. Fred Ward/Black Star; t.(in-set) William Campbell/Sygma; m.l. Stephen J. Krasemann/DRK Photo; m. Marcello Bertinetti/Photo Researchers, Inc.; m.r. Luis Villota/The Stock Market.

62: t.l. Tardos Camesi/The Stock Market; t.r. Gary Braasch/ Wheeler Pictures; m.l., m.r. Wolfgang Kaehler; b.m. Joe Viesti/ Viesti Associates; b.r. Steve Leonard/Black Star. 62–63 b. Bill O'Connor/Peter Arnold, Inc. 63: b.r. Kurt Scholz/Shostal.

68: b. Lynn Johnson/Black Star; t.l. Joe Viesti/Viesti Associates; t.m., m.r. 69 t.m. Robert Frerck/Odyssey Productions. 68–69 b. Brian Brake/Photo Researchers, Inc. 69: t.r. Marcel Isy-Schwart/ The Image Bank; m.l. John Eastcott/Yva Momatiuk/Woodfin Camp; m.r. Peter Vorlicek/The Stock Market.

ILLUSTRATION CREDITS

Cover: Gary Ciccarelli

41: m.r. Copyright © 1990 by the New York Times Company. Reprinted by permission. Illustration by Hank Iken.
36, 59, 74–75: Howard Friedman
iv–1, 12–13, 32–33, 40–41, 48–49, 54–55, 62–63, 68–69: Joe Svadlenka